HOW TO

HANDLE
Your CHILD
CUSTODY Case

A GUIDE
FOR PARENTS,
PSYCHOLOGISTS,
& ATTORNEYS

LEONARD DIAMOND, Ph.D.

PROMETHEUS BOOKS
BUFFALO, NEW YORK

92 91 90 89   4 3 2 1

Library of Congress Cataloging-in-Publication Data

Diamond, Leonard, 1937-
    How to handle your child custody case : a manual for parents, psychologists, and attorneys / Leonard Diamond.
        p.   cm.
    ISBN 0-87975-570-9
    1. Custody of children—United States. I. Title.
KF546.D5 1989
346.7301'7—dc20
[347.30617]   89-34701
                                                                          CIP

HOW TO

HANDLE
Your CHILD
CUSTODY Case

To those who love me and gracefully tolerate my long work hours; to the very competent judges, mediators, and attorneys in Ventura County who are my friends and for whom I have the highest respect; and to Curtis W., the first child I ever evaluated in a custody matter, and all of the thousands of children who have followed, each one teaching me something new about life.

Table of Contents

Introduction

This book is presented to the reader with the specific purpose of offering a comprehensive overview of the field of child custody. It is hoped that the experiences and the techniques which will be described in detail can clear up some of the difficulties that frequently appear in child custody and mediations disputes.

Perhaps the two most significant bits of advice for a parent considering child custody are:

1. Find an attorney who specializes in family law and is certified in this particular area.

All too often people will employ attorneys who are friends, relatives, or friends of friends. These lawyers may be very well-meaning, even skilled, but they are frequently involved in fields unrelated to domestic law. They will try to muddle through the difficulties in order to please their clients, but are neither well-prepared nor competent enough to handle the matter. A client will often end up seeking a more qualified attorney after the case has been thoroughly botched and his or her position irreparably damaged.

Begin at the outset with a well-trained attorney who both enjoys working in and is familiar with the field of domestic law; one who knows the correct procedures and motions. A great deal of time, energy, and money will be saved, and there will be less anxiety and tension for parents and children. An attorney who regularly deals with domestic matters has a repertoire of shortcuts, settlement plans, and skills which will prove invaluable to all concerned. I have spent many hours in courtrooms watching lawyers make inappropriate motions, cite incorrect case law, make increasingly foolish objections, and repeatedly antagonize judges with their incompetence. I have also been privileged to see expert lawyers argue their case smoothly and carefully so that all of the cogent material is presented and the court can make a competent decision. The client must take great care in selecting an attorney who is trained and can competently represent his or her position and interests.

2. Use the services of a psychologist to make a thorough evaluation of your child and family, and be certain that this psychologist has experience, insight, and legal knowledge with regard to child custody.

The area of assessment and mediation of child custody, which is muddy at best, has been made far worse by the intrusion into the field of poorly prepared clinical psychologists and other mental health professionals. Many a well-meaning but otherwise ignorant psychologist, marriage counselor, psychiatrist, or social worker has contributed unwittingly to the chaos of a custody battle, either by exhibiting a lack of understanding of the central issues, utilizing inappropriate testing procedures (or not testing at all), or producing incompetent and poorly written reports. In addition, they often prove unable to function on the witness stand under the pressures of cross-examination.

No one is better able to assist your attorney secure custody of your child than a clinical psychologist. However, it is vitally important for this specialist to be highly competent, familiar with all of the aspects of current law, and very articulate when discussing psychological matters. Only in this manner can s/he function effectively within a clinical and legal system specifically designed to make custody decisions. In court s/he will be faced with enormous pressures and responsibilities that require the utmost in careful preparation and skill, in regard to both direct and cross-examination testimony. In order to be effective in conveying the important points and enlightening the trier of fact, the psychologist must have a great deal of professional knowledge and poise.

As of this writing I have completed evaluations of more than two thousand child custody cases. Many were settled immediately after my report was issued, but a large percentage of the cases (approximately one-third) went on to formal court hearings. The techniques and the specific structured interviews which appear in this book are the fruits of necessity and have gradually emerged from the mire of my experience. This book has three specific goals: 1. to enlighten parents about the processes involved in both assessing child custody and mediating custody contracts; 2. to serve as a reference for parents, psychologists, and family law attorneys so they have an idea which psychological and evaluative procedures are appropriate to use; and 3. the most important goal of all, to protect the children who are all but lost and forgotten in the struggle.

If the reader will consider the ideas and insights that follow, it is hoped that he or she will be better able to assess not only the legal process, but the appropriateness of utilizing psychological assistance as well. An effective team approach can truly nurture rather than inhibit the growth of the children involved. Ironically, though these young people are at the center of these custody disputes, they are frequently completely overlooked. Often a long and involved hearing is completed without the judge ever having met or heard from the child or even seen what s/he looks like. In the custody process, children are not directly represented, have no real voice in determining their future, are frequently confused by the situation they are in, and are unable to influence the adults around them who are empowered to make the crucial decisions affecting their lives. Therefore, they require the protection offered by an unbiased evaluation. The objective psychologist represents a safeguard.

This book has been reviewed by clinical psychologists, attorneys, domestic court judges, mediators, and other various professional readers. It has been both applauded and criticized for the same point: nowhere here will you find any direct references or citations to specific, objective, "hard data" psychological research or literature. There are no footnotes at the bottom of every page and no bibliography. There is, of course, an emerging body of excellent research in the area of custody which certainly should not be overlooked or denied. I would strongly encourage the reader to spend time in both law and psychology libraries to search out these studies and learn as much in these fields as possible. Entering into a custody battle as a naive participant-observer is foolishly self-defeating. One should be as prepared as possible. However, at this time my specific purpose is to communicate my practical experiences, so theoretical research has no place in my book. Besides, anything ever researched or written in either legal or psychological fields has engendered both pro and con, majority and minority opinions. The methods or procedures can be questioned and the statistics used can be viewed from many different perspectives.

My goal in presenting this information is to converse with the reader about my work and experiences. I look forward to sharing insights and feedback with all those who choose to read this book, and very definitely welcome ideas, comments, feelings, philosophies, and opinions from others involved in the emotionally draining and dramatic field of child custody. Therefore, I have purposely omitted the research material and instead placed my emphasis and concentration on true life occurrences, mundane as well as exciting—the courtroom incidents and tribulations of the working legal world. This yields practical data that will help parents and legal and psychological practitioners to make more informed decisions. These are experiences that make custody work challenging, difficult, and often highly emotionally rewarding. These experiences do not readily lend themselves to quantification and to reduction into mere numbers, statistical analyses, or hard data research.

One who elects to pursue a child custody matter makes him- or herself vulnerable to a high degree of aggravation, anxiety, and perhaps even the threat of physical danger. But the satisfaction one derives from following through with personal principles—the belief that one is acting in the best interests of the child and that this is done with love and caring—clearly outweighs the negative aspects. The parent who embarks on this struggle must serve the interests of the child, and not his or her own. If not, a circus of madness ensues which makes a mockery of the justice system and victimizes the child.

Often, otherwise competent and rational adults who are locked in a litigious struggle will deteriorate into very disturbed people, especially when they are threatened with the loss of a child. When they come into my office, they express their desire to seek a custody settlement which will be in the best interests of the child. They say with great frequency that the needs of the child are paramount and that they will be happy to abide by the suggestions that grow out of the psychological evaluation. Clients will present their positions. They will also attempt to flatter the evaluator, indicating that s/he is the mutually agreed-upon expert who has been chosen by all parties concerned to help unravel the knot and supply concrete plans. Most people believe these words when they are spoken, but there always exists a hidden agenda: Since that parent has determined the needs of the child, then that parent's needs are the ones that come first. If a report is issued to the court that supports that person's ex-spouse, the evaluator and the attorney frequently receive negative calls or angry letters. In these communications the parent vents his or her anger and informs the expert that s/he is really an incompetent boob who knows nothing, is conspiring with "the other side" and should be shot where s/he stands so that s/he will not be able to mess up anyone else's life. Calm, gentle, bright, and capable parents are often transformed into angry check-bouncers under this type of stress. It is hoped that this book can provide enough insight into the process to help parents avoid such negative feelings, and encourage them to work with the system to accept plans that are truly in the best interests of their children.

1
The Referral

The Referral to the Psychologist: Using the "Team Approach"

Although psychiatrists have been accepted in courts for decades, only recently has the justice system recognized the competence and the contributions of psychologists. It is difficult to understand the reasons for this discrimination, but it probably can be attributed to the entrenched conservatism of the justice system, the political power of the medical-psychiatric community and the poor professional record of psychologists in the past. This has changed considerably of late, and it has been my experience that more and more psychologists have been appearing in court actions. Psychological testimony is now very much accepted, sought after, and recognized by the judiciary as highly valid. This is a most fortunate development for a parent involved in a custody dispute. Psychological testing that is competently performed and professionally reported can offer a rational way out of the custody morass.

Psychologists who wish to become involved in the field of custody evaluation must learn to communicate this to attorneys in the family law community. Many psychologists have reported to me that they have become involved merely by chance, because an attorney happens to be a friend or has been sent by a mutual acquaintance. Making contacts in this manner is obviously impractical, and there are far more effective procedures a psychologist can utilize to stimulate interest and receive custody referrals.

Both parents seeking to open a custody matter and psychologists who want to become involved in the field need to make contact with attorneys working in the family law area. County bar associations are usually split into divisions dealing with highly refined legal specialties, one of which is family law. In order to keep up with new techniques, laws, and literature, those in the field will likely meet on a regular basis, and one can find out about these meetings by contacting the local bar association. Family law groups usually have dinner meetings at which they hear presentations by speakers concerned with developments in child custody law and procedure. For the psychologist new to the locality, getting to know these groups is a must. A very effective method for letting these attorneys know you are available, prepared, and competent to deal with custody issues is to call the association, attend the meetings, and get to know the individual attorneys. Similarly, a parent who requires the service of a psychologist should not simply shop for one in the yellow pages, but be referred to one through his or her attorney. It is critical that the psychologist is accepted by the legal community as a reliable expert. For this reason, it is worthwhile for the psychologist to volunteer services for consultation and speaking engagements when first getting started. Attorneys, like other professionals, need to test their products, and a psychologist's initial impression with regard to his or her expertise is most important. An attorney needs a psychologist who can communicate effectively in the courtroom. A lawyer must present his or her information before a judge in a clear and concise manner.

Both the attorney and client should be aware of the psychologist's philosophy regarding child custody. A parent seeking a joint custody arrangement certainly does not want to employ a psychologist who does not believe in this process. The client should feel comfortable with his or her team. When talking to one's attorney or psychologist, one shouldn't feel overwhelmed by jargon. It is appropriate for an attorney to talk in "legalese" when in court, but the psychologist has the added burden of translating psychological terms into legal ones so that s/he can effectively get his or her points across to the judge. This is a very difficult task and demands a high degree of skill and knowledge on the part of the psychologist.

Psychologists cannot become experts in this field by simply springing upon the scene. They must develop competence in both psychological and legal areas. Learning the language is critical. Psychologists must be able to communicate efficiently with attorneys. If a lawyer calls up and says, "I am sending over an SDT for the Jones OSC re: modification," the psychologist should know that this means, "You will soon receive a paper from a process server that will tell you when you have to come to court for the Jones' family custody hearing."

Just as psychologists should take a family law course at a local law school before attempting this type of work, so should attorneys take courses in psychological testing. Such courses are often scheduled in the evening or can be taken by correspondence. They are most informative and enjoyable. Psychologists should spend time talking with attorneys and reading as much as they can about custody laws. By doing this the language will become familiar, as will the major issues prevalent in custody battles. It is also immeasurably important for both client and psychologist to spend time in a courtroom. Observing cases as they develop is the only effective way of learning courtroom procedures and routines. Thus, when the client comes to the court for his or her own case, s/he won't be intimidated by the novelty of the situation. As in any kind of preparation, regular practice over a long period is more effective than last-minute cramming. Obviously, a custody case is not something one should wait until the night before to prepare for. Time spent in court listening to legal arguments, watching witnesses being cross-examined, and learning courtroom procedures goes a long way toward demystifying the law. It is definitely a worthwhile step to take.

Many attorneys rely on psychologists and psychiatrists who come to court simply to testify for a fee. These witnesses for hire, who are often incompetent charlatans, are encountered regularly in the halls of justice. The majority of attorneys, however, seek mental health professionals who are honest, forthright, and competent. They prefer to see someone who will help to win the case by putting on a dazzling display of expertise. The attorneys willing to take a risk with an honest man or woman are usually highly skilled professionals themselves. They have great respect for an honest, competent psychologist no matter which side s/he supports and will come back again and again to utilize his or her evaluation services. Clients who are able to engage a bright, honest, competent attorney and a bright, honest, competent psychologist will get their best opportunity in court. Hiring unprofessional, incompetent, or dishonest attorneys and psychologists usually spells doom for the case—and disaster for the family.

The client watching an opposing attorney cross-examine an expert witness is frequently frightened by how vicious the process is. I have frequently been the victim of ruthless, aggressive questioning by an attorney. But though such a lawyer may lose his or her case, s/he is especially likely to call for assistance on other cases in the future. Both s/he and the psychologist know that such attacks are a common game played in the courtroom. Even if it looks as if a personal attack is taking place, this usually is not the case. And the attorney who sees the psychologist hold up under the stress and pressure of cross-examination develops a high respect for the expert's abilities, which means future referrals and more work. This is also very gratifying to the client as s/he feels that s/he has received the best representation possible. Attorneys who are beaten fair and square by a superior presentation in court are more likely to call that psychologist in the future rather than one who testifies merely for cash.

The administrative officer of the county superior court draws up a list of psychologists and psychiatrists (called alienists) who are qualified to be called upon for legal work. This involves custody and criminal assessments as well as other types of consultations required by the court. This list is supplied as a reference for judges and mediators. In order to be included on it, the mental health practitioners must write to the administrative officer and submit a complete resume or curriculum vitae along with a request to be placed on the court panel. They are also interviewed and asked to fill out a questionnaire. This alerts the judges to the individual's availability, specialties, educational, and experiential background as well as desire to assist the court in making decisions regarding child custody. When an especially difficult case arises and the judge feels that s/he requires an outside evaluation, the judge will review this list with the attorneys. They will then agree on a psychologist, stipulating that the clinician perform a study, which will be introduced as evidence subject to cross-examination. Parents involved in such a case should realize that this process should not be completed without consulting them. It is vital that the attorney and the client decide together what their specific needs are, and find an evaluator who fulfills them.

Many superior courts also have what are variously known as conciliation centers, arbitrators, or family relations investigations services. Such a department is designed either to investigate and make recommendations on custody disputes, or to actually mediate and conciliate them. This process is designed to unclog the court calendar and keep some cases from continuing on to the formal hearing process. These departments are another excellent place for finding competent and expert psychologists. They are constantly searching for outside evaluators to assist in the process as well as psychologists who are able to treat emotional and communication disturbances in families. These mediation departments are almost always flooded with cases, are usually terribly understaffed, and generally are unable to service all of the attorneys and clients requesting assistance. Because of this, they make many referrals to outside professionals in the private sector. They select their expert psychologists in very much the same way as the court administrative officer: by reviewing their resumes, conducting brief interviews, and by inquiring about the psychologist's reputation among other attorneys. The court-appointed mediator is always a good source for those seeking an expert since they consistently utilize tried-and-true professionals with whom they can communicate well.

In order for the attorney and the client to feel comfortable in making a selection, they should get a list of a few names and check with each psychologist personally, in order to find out if they will communicate with him or her well. Asking to see samples of the psychologist's work is advisable as well, and will be of much value in assessing and understanding his or her styles or biases.

Putting together a good team to work on a child custody case requires study, time, dedication, good planning, and communication with those people who are involved in the custody process on a regular basis. Both the psychological expert and the legal expert should be judged on their individual merits, their overall competence, and not least of all, their track record.

The Psychologist as an Advocate

Often an attorney will call a psychologist, stating that s/he is considering taking on a client who seeks to gain custody of a child. The attorney wishes to have an evaluation of the client and the child so that s/he can determine whether the case has merit. The attorney needs to know whether it is appropriate to take the case to court, and whether it can be won. This places the psychologist at a considerable disadvantage since s/he only has the opportunity to see one parent, and perhaps—but not always—the child. Most often it is a case in which a marriage has already disolved and the child is living with one parent and temporarily visiting the other. The noncustodial parent now requests that the matter be reopened because of some change in circumstance which s/he believes would permit persuing either sole or joint custody. This often requires that the evaluation be scheduled on a weekend rather than during normal work hours since visitation usually takes place on the weekend, which raises a very interesting ethical issue: Should a child be evaluated psychologically without the knowledge or approval of the primary custodial parent? The child, of course, will tell the primary custodial parent about the evaluation sessions, and the psychologist can then expect a threatening phone call or an angry letter from an attorney. This is most difficult and requires taking a firm stand.

It is my belief that when a parent has a child for his or her visitation period, that parent is to be considered to be the primary custodian at that time. Therefore s/he has the right to bring the child in for an evaluation (or to a physician for a checkup, or to any other medical professional). Many would argue with this position, but I feel it is entirely legitimate for a parent to have full control of a child when that child is in his or her possession and custody, temporary or not. Otherwise this totally debilitates the status of parent, and does not permit the visiting parent any say in decision-making.

Nonetheless, when a parent considers a custody suit, s/he should be prepared to accept the fact that all of the members of the family will have to be interviewed and tested. Evaluating only one parent often leads to distorted and inappropriate conclusions. One must always remember that the reports clients offer represent their own perceptions of reality. Although most parents truly believe that they are presenting the truth, their statements are by no means the whole truth.

Let's examine a worst-case scenario. A psychologist is approached and asked to evaluate a child and the child's father in preparation for a possible custody suit. The father feels that he should get custody now since he is newly remarried, has a fine house, an expensive English car, a steady, well-paying job, a new VCR, and all of the things he thinks a child "really needs" to nurture his or her growth. Testing follows, which reveals that the father is in fact somewhat dependent, and appears as a benign individual who is nevertheless prone to excessively manipulative behavior. He is still viewed as basically healthy and does not demonstrate anything that would contra-indicate fairly good parenting skills. The child shows good mental health and has a fairly strong identification with and attachment for the father. A report stating these facts is written, sent to the attorney, and nothing further is heard for the next six months. Suddenly a subpoena appears requiring testimony in court.

This is the worst possible position for a psychologist to be in since s/he has been manipulated into the role of advocate for one parent. S/he is now subject to cross-examination from the other parent's attorney. This attorney asks immediately how much time was spent with the mother prior to writing the report outlining the father-child relationship. The answer, of course, is that she was not seen at all. Her attorney, with a smirk, says, "Doctor, do you mean to tell this court that you have made decisions and reached conclusions with regard to the custody of this minor child and yet you never saw the mother? You saw only one parent?" After receiving an affirmative reply, the attorney then proceeds to introduce evidence through hypothetical questions. Did the psychologist know that the father has been accused of child molestation, spent two years in a drug rehabilitation center, was in prison for four years on bunko charges, and is currently involved in his second bankruptcy? That the mother is a hard working grocery store clerk who cares for her child diligently and does go out in the evening with friends approximately twice each week? And that father wants to have custody in order to avoid making the monthly child support payments to the mother?

What now, doctor?

To study only one side of a custody matter is obviously dangerous and is rarely appropriate. Often, only a small sample of important facts are revealed and any records will be offered on a very selective basis. It is possible both the attorney and the psychologist are denied this information, or that the attorney and client will feed the psychologist only the information they feel would be supportive to the their case. This is a foolish tactic, since the opposing attorney (unless s/he is totally incompetent) will inevitably try to impeach the testimony of the psychologist.

The expert will be immediately dispatched from the courtroom with his or her credibility destroyed.

If a psychologist is to evaluate just one parent, it should be done only under specific conditions—if the other parent refuses to be cooperative, or if the judge does not order an evaluation. In such a case, I have set down specific rules that will clarify the circumstances and keep everyone as honest as possible. A definitive decision regarding custody should never be made under these conditions and a psychologist should not offer a report if either or both conditions apply. I utilize a disclaimer in my report which states this explicitly. This informs the court that I am offering data but that no decisions should be made based on the data since it is obviously incomplete. The following is a sample of this type of disclaimer:

> This report is based on contact only with Mr. Smith and his child. It does not include any first-hand data concerning Mrs. Smith. The only information on the family or ex-spouse has been supplied to me by Mr. Smith and is considered to be hearsay. In addition, my conclusions regarding parenting skills and abilities are based on office contact, psychological testing, and the specific data supplied to me by Mr. Smith and by his attorney, Mr. (or Ms.) Jones. Therefore, I am not able to make any definitive statement regarding custody but only to indicate that this individual is or is not capable of good parenting skills at this time. These direct conclusions are based on the limited sample of data available to me.

Clients and attorneys who refuse a report with the type of disclaimer described above are clearly seeking a biased evaluation. It is important for anyone who wants custody of a child to realize that the only successful and correct approach is to be straightforward, honest, ethical, and professional with the court. The "Doctrine of Unclean Hands" should apply not only to plaintiffs and petitioners but also to experts. This doctrine refers to an individual who uses the courts inappropriately (like kidnapping a child to another state and then filing and receiving custody in that new state), and it has no relief in equity. The attorney or psychologist who attempts to manipulate the court with biased data because s/he has been offered a fat fee is similarly sullying the legal process with unclean hands.

A client who truly cares about the children and an attorney who is ethical and honest, coupled with a psychologist who has all the information possible, can be a very effective team. A case can be won far more easily by such a partnership. It must be understood that this team should strive to seek conditions that are in the best interests and welfare of the children. This necessitates a thorough disclosure of all information, documents, and declarations relevant to the case. An attorney who is willing to work in this manner will let his or her client know that everything must come out, that the client must "let the chips fall where they may," and trust in the work of the team.

The Psychologist as an Appointee of the Court

It is perhaps best for the client and the attorney to have a psychologist who is appointed by the court. This implies that both parents and their attorneys agree that a professional evaluation is necessary and helpful. The judge or mediator will present them with a list of the competent evaluators and a mutually agreeable one is selected. This is an enviable position for a psychologist to be in. No matter who is ordered to pay for the testing, the psychologist has the opportunity to truly represent the best interests of the child since everyone has agreed that s/he is an impartial observer. Even after a report is written and filed, the parent on the losing side retains the right to find another expert more supportive of his or her position who is prepared to refute the findings. However, as a rule, the appointed expert, who was retained by the judge with the informed consent and blessings of attorneys on both sides, carries far more weight with the court. It then becomes obvious that any other psychologist who is brought in is just there to attempt to distort the information. Such tactics usually upset and anger the judge as well as reflect negatively on the attorney who uses them.

If there is a family investigator or mediator associated with the court, s/he may make the referral directly, which will then be approved by the judge. In a particularly bitter and divisive case, the judge will often refer directly to the mediator rather than involve everyone in a protracted battle. The mediator is a well trained professional familiar with psychology who will interview attorneys and clients on both sides. Many mediators now hold both psychological and legal degrees. In individual and joint sessions held in the mediator's office, the facts are gathered without taking up valuable court time and a temporary custody order is formulated and agreed upon. This temporary order will remain in effect until a thorough evaluation takes place and then another court date will be set for a full and complete hearing. It is also possible for a court-sponsored evaluation to be requested by the attorney of one of the parents, the advantage of this being that the entire record is made available for study: the psychologist has the opportunity to examine everything, including depositions, declarations, court decisions, previous evaluations, school records, pleadings, reports from other agencies, and the original filing documents. The court now has a psychologist's report which is far more responsible and valuable, since it takes everything into account. I would strongly suggest that this approach be utilized rather than having an independent psychologist be employed by only one side, at the risk of creating a distracting, not to mention divisive, courtroom atmosphere.

The Psychologist Working as a Representative of the Child

A notion frequently lost in the heat of a custody battle is that the process of mediation, testing, and evaluation is put into motion for one goal: to protect the best interests and welfare of the child. This ideal is the aim of the custody process, but unfortunately, the reality frequently falls far short. Part of the reason is the very adversarial nature of courtroom procedures. Attorneys are obligated to fight for their clients's interests, which aren't necessarily those of the child. Attorneys can only trust and believe that their clients are accurately representing the facts and the children's best interests. Additionally, they run the risk of getting so wound up in winning a case that they lose sight of what is actually best for the child.

Theoretically, the court represents the best interests of the child. It is the judge's job as the trier of fact to cut through huge thickets of contradiction, lies, inflammatory testimony, and other evidence in order to render a just decision. That this decision inevitably has a profound effect on the child's life places a great deal of stress and anxiety on the judge. In addition, the judge is often hampered by strict definitions of law, evidence codes which may not permit all of the facts to be considered (or even to be known), and his or her own unwitting biases and prejudices. Each person brings his or her own humanity and limitations to the situation, including the psychological evaluator.

It is impossible to enter such a situation chaste, virginal, and totally without bias, but one can be more clear if one remembers that the goal is to represent the child and to make only those decisions that will enhance the life of the child. The court-appointed psychologist owes no allegiance to any side and operates as a free agent. S/he is the child's advocate, the most important and possibly the most influential person in that child's life at that moment. It is the psychologist who serves as the child's counsel in these proceedings, except in the rare case that a judge will actually appoint an independent attorney to represent the interests of the child. This is an unusual prodecure, and is seldom employed. When the child does not have his or her own attorney it falls on the psychologist to take on this role. Even though the case focuses on the child, s/he is usually conspicuously absent from the courtroom proceedings.

For a psychologist, representing a child can be an anxious but also highly exciting experience. The psychologist has a great deal of freedom to say all that s/he wants the court to hear. As an expert witness the psychologist may elaborate as fully as s/he wishes since the court makes it very difficult for an attorney to restrict the testimony of an expert. In a well run courtroom, no attorney will be permitted to restrict an expert to "yes or no" answers. The expert has the opportunity to fully explain all of the dynamics of the case and thus give the child his or her own special opportunity to be heard. All the psychological material relevant to the case may be freely aired. In addition, having tested the parents, the expert is also able to address their individual strengths and weaknesses as well as their capacity to raise their children.

As the psychological evaluator in a custody case I always inform the child of my role as his or her advocate in court. I let the child know that I will be talking to the judge and both lawyers about his or her needs, desires, and feelings. After completing a highly structured interview and testing session, I frequently ask the child for any additional information the judge ought to know. Children see this as a very important source of emotional support, which helps them to feel more sucure in the testing session. In court I make it a point to quote the child frequently so that the judge gets a flavor of the child's world. This helps all concerned parties to see the custody difficulty through the eyes of the child rather than those of the parents. The parents need to hear these words and respect the fact that the child has specific needs and rights which must be considered.

2

Current Child Custody Law

Historical Overview of General Custody Law

Historically, the early English courts permitted only recognition of the rights of the father in cases dealing with the custody of minor children. The father's rights took precedence over the mother's because all family members were considered the property of the father. His ability to claim his children as chattel went unchallenged and was upheld through the years with great consistency. In the early 1800s, however, new philosophies were introduced. The courts began to recognize that it was appropriate for infant children (those considered below the age of maturity) to be placed in the custody of their mothers. In order for the mother to accomplish this, she had to petition the court. Although the trend still favored the father in most cases, in many instances the mother's rights to the child were upheld. The English courts made these assignments of custody to the mother during the child's "tender years"—defined loosely as under the age of twelve.

It was the English Court of Chancery that began to understand the need to concentrate on the best interests of the child.

This court undertook to place the decision with regard to custody as a factor of the child's best interests and welfare rather than the assumed rights of the parents, and would not hesitate to take the child from the father and place him or her in the custody of the mother. However, the Court of Chancery was utilized only when there was specific property or wealth registered in the child's name. The English system had two very different and distinct sets of rules: one for wealthy, property-owning children who were permitted to have their best interests recognized; and one for children of the lower classes who were always assumed to be the property of their fathers.

In the United States, the standard method of obtaining custody was to institute habeas corpus proceedings, which were brought by the parent who wanted to obtain custody from the other. Habeas corpus literally means "Give me the body" of the child. In this type of legal action the courts had the option of utilizing the rule of the English Courts of Chancery, thereby putting aside the rights of either parent to custody. They attempted to follow the rule in the best interests of the child; however, it was generally assumed that the mother was the better parent. Over the years, courts established the tradition and formal precedent of placing minor children in the custody of the mother. Only in recent years has the area of custody undergone changes to recognize the father's ability to parent an infant child. But for the most part, the prevailing feeling in this country has been that when younger children are concerned, women are more loving, competent, and able to exercise parental care than men.

Courts have also permitted cooperating parents to establish their own custody agreements. However, the court is charged with the responsibility of invalidating these agreements if they are found to go against the best interests of the child. In addition, most courts will presume that the child's best interests are better served by a parent than by a distant relative or someone outside the family. If another relative or outsider petitions for the custody of the child and is judged equally capable as a parent, still the preference will almost always go to a parent. The objection to the rule that custody should be awarded to a parent carries the suggestion that the interests of the child are being subordinated to the interests of the parent. However, it is widely held that this is not so, that this rule serves to define the area of the parent's responsibility for maintaining the welfare of the child.

The guiding shibboleth currently used by the courts in most custody disputes is the rule of "the best interests of the child." There are many criteria which the courts consider in making this difficult determination. These include: fitness of the parents; their finances; their health; their social positions; their ability to share custody; the age of child; voiced preferences of the child; religion; race; and mental health of all concerned. In the past courts have operated fast and loose with these criteria and only recently have state legislative bodies actually formulated laws that guarantee adherence to the "best interests" rule.

Review of Current United States Custody Law

Child custody laws were ignored for decades throughout the United States. In the early 1970s, the emergence of the women's movement, equal rights laws, and changing value systems forced many state legislators to consider rewriting the custody laws. As mothers entered the work force it soon became apparent that fathers were taking on and enjoying more and more of an active parenting role. This led to father's rights groups who concentrated their efforts at lobbying the lawmakers and, eventually, affected changes in the wording and emphasis of the existing custody statutes. Prior to this time the financial support of the child was primarily the sole obligation of the father. The initial changes obligated both the mother and father to child support responsibilities. The courts began to consider the respective financial positions of both parents so that each could begin to make a legitimate and realistic financial contribution to the future of their child.

As the legislators investigated new positions and ideas with regard to parenting, the previously accepted gender requirements began to dissolve. Ongoing research and new data convinced many lawmakers that one did not necessarily have to be a woman to be an effective parent. The concept of "mothering" gave way to the concept of "parenting" and the courts opened their eyes to the fact that mothers were not automatically more effective parents. In fact, for many years most of the states had existing statutes which provided equal rights of custody for both parents. However, these laws were generally ignored by the courts, and the mother prevailed in virtually all decisions regarding contested custody matters. A growing number of states provided that there should be no presumptions favoring either parent because of their gender. These states attempted to equalize parental rights to custody. They include Delaware, Texas, Wisconsin, Minnesota, Nebraska, New Hampshire, and the District of Columbia. Other states handled the issue of desexing custody by altering their state constitutions to include ERA statutes, such as Alaska, Colorado, Connecticut, Hawaii, Illinois, Louisiana, Maryland, Massachusetts, Montana, New Mexico, Pennsylvania, Utah, Virginia, Washington, and Wyoming.

As statutes were altered, a number of specific issues arose and were incorporated in the new laws. These included: the age and gender of the child; the desires of both the child and the parents; an examination of the existing interactions and of the specific relationships among the children, parents, and siblings; the child's adjustment to areas of his or her home, school, and community environments; and mental and physical health of all of the parties in the action. These more encompassing guidelines are found in the laws of Arizona, Delaware, the District of Columbia, Florida, Illinois, Indiana, Kentucky, Louisiana, Michigan, Minnesota, Missouri, Montana, Nebraska, Ohio, and Vermont. They were derived from the federal Uniform Marriage and Divorce Act and were elaborated, modified, or revised by the specific legislatures, or incorporated entirely into the new statues. In addition to these areas, there arose a new awareness by courts of the need for psychological investigations in custody cases. Judges began to seek corroborative information and wisely conceded some of their arbitrary decision-making powers. Investigative, mediation, and conciliation bodies were established to assist the court in making these difficult decisions. Many states also recognized the child's lack of representation and enacted additional statutes that permit the child specific representation, such as his or her own attorney or a guardian ad litem.

Many states have adopted the Uniform Child Custody Jurisdiction Act. These states include Alaska, California, Colorado, Delaware, Florida, Hawaii, Idaho, Indiana, Iowa, Maryland, Michigan, Minnesota, Montana, New York, North Dakota, Ohio, Oregon, Pennsylvania, Wisconsin, and Wyoming. The basic purpose of this act is to discourage continued controversies over the custody of children and to ensure that each child has a stable home environment. It also deals with the abduction of children and is designed to promote interstate assistance in adjudicating custody matters. It promotes cooperation with all courts so that the custody decree can be rendered in the state which can best decide the case in the best interests of the child. In addition, it assures that any litigation must take place in the state in which the child and his family have the closest connection and personal relationships. The Act deters abductions, unilateral removals of children, and does not permit relitigation in new states, but rather is designed to facilitate the enforcement of decrees in other states; it does not allow one state to usurp jurisdiction over another. Thus, this complex act is designed to force the parents to deal with the case in the most appropriate court, accept the judgment of that court, and not attempt to use the courts in other states inappropriately.

California Custody Law: A Model

The major portion of the California law regarding child custody is covered in section 4600 of the California Civil Code, Title 4, CUSTODY OF CHILDREN. This law has been modified a number of times and more progressive sections continue to be added.

As a result, California has some of the most sophisticated and enlightened custody laws in the country. They serve as a model for progressive humanization in the field. While they might not be perfect, they represent a definite solution to some problems and a sound beginning approach to the resolution of others. The current law covers the following sections:

Section 4600: Custody of children; order of preference; award to nonparent.

Section 4600.1: Petition for temporary custody order.

Section 4600.2: Order directing noncustodial parent to pay child support.

Section 4600.5: Joint custody of minor child.

Section 4600.6: Trials involving joint custody.

Section 4601: Visitation rights.

Section 4601.5: Visitation conditioned on presence of third party.

Section 4602: Custody investigation and report.

Section 4603: Action for custody without dissolution.

Section 4604: Whereabouts unknown, action to locate.

Section 4604.5: Verification that child has been reported missing or abducted.

Section 4605: Whereabouts unknown, payment of expenses.

Section 4606: Appointment of counsel for child, payment.

Section 4607: Mediation necessitated in issues involving child custody or visitation.

Section 4607.1: Findings and declarations, standards for mediation of custody and visitation cases.

Section 4607.2: Separate meetings with mediator in cases with past history of domestic violence.

Section 4608: Best interests of child as including consideration of health, safety, and welfare.

Section 4609: Family reunification services in connection with child custody or visitation rights proceeding.

Section 4610: Award of custody or unsupervised visitation, finding of no significant risk to child required.

It is apparent that these laws are quite complex and highly inclusive. It is critical that anyone involved in a custody issue, from a parental or professional view, be thoroughly familiar with the laws of his or her state. California law illustrates many of the often utilized general principles of custody. A discussion of sections 4600, 4600.5, and 4607 follows.

Section 4600 begins by directly addressing the fact that children need both parents. "The Legislature finds and declares that it is the public policy of this state to assure minor children of frequent and continuing contact with both parents after the parents have separated or dissolved their marriage, and to encourage parents to share the rights and responsibilities of child rearing in order to effect this policy." The section ends by stating: "This section establishes neither a preference nor a presumption for or against joint legal custody, joint physical custody, or sole custody, but allows the court and the family the widest discretion to choose a parenting plan that is in the best interests of the child or children."

The body of 4600 further elaborates that it is the responsibility of the court to make an assignment with regard to custody when the child is a minor, and to hear the wishes and desires of that child if the child "is of sufficient age and capacity to reason so as to form an intelligent preference as to custody."

The court is bound to "consider and give due weight to the wishes of the child." This is an interesting and difficult section to interpret since no actual or specific age distinction is offered. Because of this, an evaluating psychologist has an added responsibility as well as a great deal of latitude in indicating to the judge if a child is mature enough for his or her statements to be considered. Most courts have a generally accepted but unwritten standard that determines the age of reason. For most judges this is generally set at eleven or twelve, although it has been set as low as eight and as high as fourteen. Obviously, there is no hard and fast rule for determining the age of reason, and the attorney and psychologist should make a point to alert the judge, in a report or in court, whether the child should be interviewed in chambers. Rarely should a child be called to take the witness stand, since this can often be highly traumatic. A child should not have to testify publicly for or against a parent. For such reasons, a private interview is more appropriate.

Many judges are reluctant to do even this because they feel they lack the expertise to interview children. However, some judges enjoy dealing with a child and are most willing and eager to know his or her wishes and desires. In these cases, the evaluating psychologist and attorney can play an important role by supporting the interview so that the child can be directly represented. Although it is important to spare a child the stress and anxiety of the courtroom, it is equally important to impress upon the judge that a real life is involved and not just a case number. Bright and aware five year olds have the right to be heard if they are able to articulate their feelings and desires. To allow children the right to express themselves could make an enormous difference in court decisions.

Section 4600 goes on to state that custody should be awarded in a specific order of preference according to the best interests of the child. This order is quoted from the civil code as follows:

> 1. To both parents jointly pursuant to Section 4600.5 or to either parent. In making an order for custody to either parent, the court shall consider, among other factors, which parent is more likely to allow to child or children frequent and continuing contact with the noncustodial parent, and shall not prefer a parent as custodian because of that parent's sex. The court, in its discretion, may require the parents to submit to the court a plan for the implementation of the custody order.
> 2. If to neither parent, to the person or persons in whose home the child has been living in a wholesome and stable environment.
> 3. To any other person or persons deemed by the court to be suitable and able to provide adequate and proper care and guidance for the child.

This section presents the distinct possibility that the custody of the child may be awarded to someone other that his or her parents. However, the court must be thoroughly and completely satisfied that an award of custody to one or both parents would be damaging or detrimental to the child for such a decision to be made. Additionally, an award to a nonparent must be designed to serve the best interests and welfare of the child. This section also protects the parents by providing that negative allegations need not appear in the pleadings, and the court may, at its own discretion, exclude the public and maintain a closed hearing.

Of the numerous evaluations that I have conducted, I have recommended for nonparents in only four cases. In each of these cases the parents were both far too disturbed or intellectually unable to care for the children properly. The custody was awarded to grandparents, aunts, and uncles with visitation for the parents. A comprehensive custody evaluation should certainly take into consideration significant relatives who may be an integral part of the child's life—especially when the child is residing with someone other than a parent. When arranging for this type of evaluation it is important for the attorney to have the psychologist establish the appointments close together. When different family names are involved there is too much potential for confusion. I have seen attorneys and psychologists heavily involved in a complex custody case unable to recall which grandparent went with which family. Obviously, considerable care must be taken to keep everyone in order and reduce confusion.

Section 4600.5 made a significant change in the entire thrust of the California child custody law. It speaks to the legislature's sincere and dogmatic conviction that a child should not be denied either parent if at all possible and if appropriate to the circumstances. The code section is quoted as follows:

(a) There shall be a presumption, affecting the burden of proof, that joint custody is in the best interests of a minor child where the parents have agreed to an award of joint custody or so agree in open court at a hearing for the purpose of determining the custody of a minor child of the marriage.

(b) Upon the application of either parent, joint custody may be awarded at the discretion of the court in other cases. For the purpose of assisting the court in making a determination whether an award of joint custody is appropriate under this subdivision, the court may direct that an investigation be conducted pursuant to the provisions of Section 4602.

(c) Whenever a request for joint custody is granted or denied, the court, upon the request of any party, shall state in its decision the reasons for granting or denying the request. A statement that joint physical custody is, or is not, in the best interests of the child shall not be sufficient to meet the requirements of this subdivision.

(d) For the purposes of this part:
(1) "Joint custody" means joint physical custody and joint legal custody.
(2) "Sole physical custody" means that a child shall reside with and under the supervision of one parent, subject to the power of the court to order visitation.
(3) "Joint physical custody" means that each of the parents shall have significant periods of physical custody. Joint physical custody shall be shared by the parents in such a way so as to assure a child of frequent and continuing contact with both parents.
(4) "Sole legal custody" means that one parent shall have the right and the responsibility to make the decisions relating to the health, education, and welfare of a child.
(5) "Joint legal custody" means that both parents shall share the right and the responsibility to make the decisions relating to the health, education, and welfare of a child.

(e) In making an order of joint legal custody, the court shall specify the circumstances under which the consent of both parents is required to be obtained in order to exercise legal control of the child and the consequences of the failure to obtain mutual consent. In all other circumstances, either parent acting alone may exercise legal control of the child. An order of joint legal custody shall not be construed to permit an action that is inconsistent with the physical custody order unless the action is expressly authorized by the court.

(f) In making an order of joint physical custody, the court shall specify the right of each parent to the physical control of the child in sufficient detail to enable a parent deprived of that control to implement laws for relief of child snatching and kidnapping.

(g) In making an order for custody with respect to both parents, the court may award joint legal custody without awarding joint physical custody.

(h) In making an order of joint physical custody or joint legal custody, the court may specify one parent as the primary caretaker of the child and one home as the primary home of the child, for the purpose of determining eligibility for public assistance.

(i) Any order for joint custody may be modified or may be terminated upon the petition of one or both parents or on the court's own motion if it is shown that the best interests of the child require modification or termination of the order. The court shall state in its decision the reasons for modification or termination of the joint custody order if either parent opposes the modification or termination order.

(j) Any order for the custody of a minor child of a marriage entered by a court in this state or any other state may, subject to the jurisdictional requirements set forth in sections 5152 and 5163, be modified at any time to an order of joint custody in accordance with the provisions of this section.

(k) In counties having a conciliation court, the court or the parties may, at any time, pursuant to local rules of court, consult with the conciliation court for the purpose of assisting the parties to formulate a plan for the implementation of the custody order or to resolve any controversy which has arisen in the implementation of a plan for custody.

(l) Notwithstanding any other provisions of law, access to records and information pertaining to a minor child, including but not limited to medical, dental, and school records, shall not be denied to a parent because such parent is not the child's custodial parent.

The California legislature, in adapting this most enlightened and highly specific position, has offered a law that ensures that joint custody will be considered in each situation. Most judges are now supporting and considering joint custody whenever possible. This is especially true for joint legal custody, which is clearly a different concept from joint physical custody. Joint legal custody orders are made with a high degree of frequency not only to honor the law but often as a face-saving device so that both parents can claim to have custody. Under ideal conditions this should guarantee both parents the opportunity to have input into the growth and development of the child. Both should have equal opportunity to help make the major decisions affecting the child's future. Unfortunately, all too often joint legal custody in practice enables the one parent with physical custody of the child to make all major decisions unilaterally, while denying the parent with the usual alternate weekend and holiday visitations real involvement in the decisions.

One would assume that a truly meaningful joint custody agreement would require not only joint legal but also joint physical custody. The actual meaning of joint physical custody is also ambiguous; it certainly does not dictate that the child's time must be split exactly on an equal basis between both parents. Many aspects of the law are not specific or clear on this point, and there are a number of hand-picked judicial committees in numerous states across the country that are attempting to draft more complete definitions. Unfortunately, this might have the consequence of hampering psychologists and professional mediators in the writing of custody contract agreements. These contract agreements often serve to keep the parents from continuing the bitter courtroom battles. Such agreements are in the best interests of the child, for a successful mediator can shift the focus of the parents's attention away from their own needs to those of the child. Parents who are willing, eager, and cooperative can be highly creative in designing their own particular coparenting, time-sharing, joint physical custody agreement precisely *because* the law is ambiguous. These agreements are discussed in a later chapter.

Section 4607 has had a strong influence on the custody field. It was added to ensure that all possibilities for a joint custody agreement be offered to the parents by stipulating that all cases involving custody and/or visitation matters must be referred to a mediator before the court takes any specific action. As the mediation process became mandatory, the number of joint custody awards increased and a great deal of pressure was taken off judges. The mediators played an additional role by consulting with the attorneys involved, partly so that they would accept the new process but also in order that they would themselves offer information that would lend credence to the mediator's recommendations. The utilization of the mediation process has served to make judges more sensitive to the meaning of joint custody. Parents are afforded another opportunity to give and receive information as well as get a better idea of their possible options. The law has offered parents the services of a skilled individual who can assist in the making of compromises. Mediators bring reason into the actual forging of agreements, lessen the need for advocates, and focus attention on the needs of the children. As the mediation process continues and becomes more sophisticated, it is my fervent hope that it will completely replace the formal court custody hearing.

When conducting a child custody evaluation, the mediator or psychologist must carefully consider the spirit of the law. Even when it appears that one parent should take physical custody, the mediator must look for ways in which a joint custody arrangement can be reached. This way, a child may be assured the benefits of a living, ongoing relationship with both a mother and father. In cases in which I recommend sole custody of one parent or joint legal custody with physical custody to one parent, I very carefully spell out a specific visitation schedule that is as liberal and varied as possible. The child has the right to maintain contact with both parents as long as they are caring people and will not harm him or her.

Many state legislatures are now following the California lawmakers by attempting to limit the domestic court judge to joint legal and joint physical custody as the primary alternatives. With mediation services, conciliation services, court-ordered in-house evaluations by family relations investigators, and outside evaluations conducted by private psychologists, a child receives closer scrutiny and looks forward to a brighter, happier future.

3

The Evaluation

DTACC Structured Interview-Parents

The DTACC (Diamond Technique for the Assessment of Child Custody) Structured Interview for Parents is presented at this point to acquaint parents, attorneys, and psychologists with areas that are critical in an investigation and child custody evaluation. Parents should be prepared to discuss all of the areas covered so that their psychologists can get a thorough look at family dynamics and the lives of the people involved. Although this interview covers a wide scope, it nevertheless cannot capture the entire range of data. It is a product of practical experience that serves to gather information specific to the problem areas one must consider in making a custody recommendation. As parents read this interview it might be helpful to answer the questions as a practice exercise to stimulate thinking preparatory to the actual evaluation. A discussion of the use and purposes of the interview follows this section.

DTACC Structured Interview-Parents

Date _____

Name _____
(Parent, Stepparent, Grandparent, Other)
Age _____ Soc.Sec.# _____
Current address _____
_____

With whom living at present _____
_____

Home phone (___) _____ Business phone (___) _____
Business address _____
_____

Birthdate _____ Birthplace _____
_____

Current Issue (Sole Custody, Vistation, Joint Custody)

I know that you have a great deal to say, and I will give you ample opportunity to tell me everything. I do wish to structure this interview so that I can get all the information I need to offer the court so that appropriate decisions can be made in this matter. At this time I would like you to discuss only the specific issue with which we are dealing. Can you please tell me:

1. Why has this issue come up now?

2. Whose idea is it to bring this issue up now and what do you think are the motives for bringing it up at all?

3. What do you want to happen and why?

4. What has the situation been like up to now with regard to the child?

5. Describe your feelings about the way things have been going under the current arrangement. In what way is it right or wrong?

6. Is there any way that you and your ex-spouse can come to a compromise with regard to this issue? What would you suggest as a possible compromise?

_____

7. What is your attorney's name? _____

8. Your attorney's phone number? _____

9. Your attorney's address? _____
_____

10. How many times have you been to court with this issue?

11. Dates of court hearings?

12. Have you had other attorneys before this one? How many and why?

13. What orders have been made by the judge with regard to custody, support, visitation, contempt, etc.?

14. Who brought each of these actions? When? Why?

15. How do you feel about the decisions that have been made and about how the situation has progressed to this point?

_____

Marriage

1. When were you married (this time)?

2. How old were you at the time of this marriage?

3. How old was your spouse at the time of this marriage?

4. How did you meet?

5. How long did you date prior to marriage?

6. What was your dating relationship like?

7. What do you think went wrong in your marriage?

8. Who was responsible for the major part of the parenting during your marriage?

9. Describe your role with regard to the children.

10. Describe your spouse's role with regard to the children.

11. Give a brief history of your previous marriage(s).

12. Are there any children from previous marriages? Names? Ages?

13. Describe your continuing contact with these children.

14. Child-support payments? How much? How often?

15. Are you dating anyone now? Living with someone? Remarried? Describe this person and the current relationship.

Occupation

1. Current occupation.

2. How long have you been at this job?

3. Specific work activities.

4. Current salary.

5. Previous occupations, by date; job activities.

6. Current financial assets.

7. Current financial debts.

8. In what way do you hope to advance in your job?

9. Do you need any specific education to maintain or move ahead in your occupation? If yes, what?

10. Do you expect to remain in this particular type of work indefinitely?

11. If not, what kind of occupation would you like to have and when do you hope to have it?

12. What is your spouse's occupation?

13. How do you feel about your spouse's occupation?

Education

1. History of previous education: schools, dates, academic achievements.

2. What did you enjoy most in school and why?

3. What did you enjoy least in school and why?

_____

Current Relationship with Child(ren)

1. Name and age of child(ren).

2. School child attends.

3. Grade.

4. Name of teacher(s).

5. How does child do in school? Grades?

6. What are child's specific academic strengths?

7. What are child's specific academic weaknesses?

8. Describe your relationship with your child.

9. What activities do you especially enjoy with your child?

10. What activities does your child enjoy doing with your spouse?

11. What are your child's special traits, abilities, or skills?

12. Why do you feel that you are the best custodial parent for this child?

13. Why would your spouse not be the best parent?

14. Do you feel that it would be in the best interests of the child to be shared between both parents?

15. Why do you feel this way?

16. What have you told your child with regard to the issues of custody and visitation?

17. What has the child said to you about custody and visitation?

18. Why do you think your child feels this way?

_____

The Future

1. What do you want in the future for yourself, your family?

2. Is there anything that I did not ask you that you would like to tell me about? Please be certain that we did not leave anything out that you feel is important and that you had expected to discuss.

_____

Descriptions of Parent

General physical appearance and hygiene.

Facial expression.

Range of emotion and interview affect.

Anxiety level.

Cooperativeness.

Speech.

Manipulativeness.

Social skills.

Body movements.

Humor, use of sarcasm.

Intellect.

Insight level.

Judgment level.

Orientation (person, place, time).

Information recall.

Small-detail awareness.

Compulsiveness.

Planning skills.

Creativity.

Legal savvy.

Consistency.

Anger at spouse.

Ability to express feelings.

Sensitivity to own needs.

Sensitivity to and acceptance of others.

Sexuality, seductiveness.

Denial mechanisms.

Truth-telling.

Test cooperation.

Psychological sophistication.

Independence.

Affection skills.

Narcissism.

Survival skills.

Financial skills.

General self-image.

Personal depth.

Reality level of future plans.

Imagination.

Action orientation.

Desire for child.

General Emotional health.

Evaluating the Parent: The Use of the DTACC Structured Interview and Other Tests

The DTACC Structured Interview is just one method of conducting a custody evaluation. Every clinician has his or her own style of gathering data developed from his or her own experience. This interview is not designed to be used as a paper and pencil questionnaire. A custody evaluation should *never* be conducted through the use of fill-in questionnaires. Any psychologist who operates this way does not recognize the enormous responsibility inherent in making custody decisions. Data should always be collected in face-to-face, one-to-one clinical interviews. This way, a relationship is developed, follow-up questions can be asked, the subject's veracity can be assessed. Any question in an interview can stimulate another, and the clinician must be alert to the necessity of following up lines of questioning. Research has demonstrated that psychologists can be notoriously unreliable judges of whether someone is telling the truth, but a face-to-face interview gives one the opportunity to observe body language, tone of voice, facial expression, and the individual's manner of responding. If these phenomena are not observed directly, one is left with only a simple actuarial data collection method which might as well have been done by a machine.

Far too many clinicians rely exclusively on paper and pencil fill-in tests to gather clinical data and spend almost no time actually interacting with the client. It is vitally important that a psychologist have a thorough and detailed rapport with the client. I have been in court many times when an opposing mental health professional has been questioned on this very point. When a clinician submits a report and then blithely states that only ten or fifteen minutes were spent with the client, the credibility of his or her testimony is easily called into question. In fact, it is always wise to know how much time was spent with one's client. And if the opposing side has hired its own psychologist, it's a good idea to put that question to him or her as well.

The DTACC Structured Interview is meant as a guideline for a clinician interviewing a parent. It offers an orderly method for collecting data which may help influence a custody or visitation decision. At the time of the evaluation, a concerned parent is usually anxious and fearful, and may ramble in a disorganized manner. The parent may have a great deal of bitterness and anger which must be vented in order for reasonable and useful data to surface. It is the responsibility of the interviewer to help the parent to order this data so that s/he can present the best possible case. A great deal of time is saved this way, as information can be elicited in a form that will help the evaluator to write a clear and cogent report. It is critical to uncover differences in attitudes, parenting skills, and personal history, as well as the grievances that exist between the parents (which are often the real issue). It is vital to learn whether the parent has adequate resources, insight, plans, and judgment to raise a child on his or her own.

The DTACC Structured Interview is designed to cover nine major areas:

1. General Information. This section is included to elicit basic personal data. It is especially useful in record keeping and can easily be transcribed onto ledger sheets or entered in a computer for history or billing purposes.

2. Perceptions of the Current Issue. It is almost impossible to find an amicable dissolution or custody agreement. The very fact that an evalutation is being requested indicates a conflict between the parents. Anger, jealousy, threats, and tension are the norm rather than the exception. Parents accuse each other of negative behavior, heap invective on one another, and have even been known to slash each other's tires. Each side wants to win the case, which means winning the children.

But how does the parent actually view the issue of custody or visitation? It is highly useful to assess what the parent actually wants and why the parent feels custody is being fought over at this time. Often it becomes obvious that issues of support or property settlement are the primary ones. The custody issue is frequently raised as a device to apply pressure to the ex-spouse in disputes over property. The unspoken terms may be something like: "You give me my pension and property, and I will give you the kids and allow you to live in the house." These hidden motives can be brought to the surface with careful and structured questioning.

3. Information Regarding Previous and Current Court Actions. Custody cases that drag on for years are very different from first-time situations. Parents who are dedicated to despising each other enjoy the fight and care little about the children; their major interest is in striking out against each other. These people are in and out of court on a regular basis. They will use whatever means they have available and will bring continuous actions such as contempt, modifications of support, and modifications of custody and/or visitation schedules. Such cases are annoyances to the court as well as to the psychologist and attorney, who must keep updating their data for court apearances. It is easy to get caught up in these protracted struggles, and be forced to become an advocate.

These parents often have a long list of former attorneys. Sometimes they exhaust their finances and have to go into court on a pro per basis (representing themselves). The evaluator should examine these past court actions carefully if s/he is considering entering into the dispute again. It is difficult sometimes to discriminate between the dogged determination of a concerned parent and litigious vengeance. Every time a psychologist is contacted for a new action, it is assumed (by the attorney) that the psychologist's opinion will be consistent with his or her original one. The present situation, however, may not be consistant with the past, forcing the psychologist to retest all of the major parties and write a new report.

4. Marriage Data. Many custody cases are complicated by a history of previous marriages or by the presence of new spouses or live-ins. Sometimes a past marriage that involves other children is discovered. I have come across many cases in which these other children have been totally forsaken or given up for adoption. The parent (who may have a vasectomy or tied tubes) suddenly realizes that these children are his or her only legacy to the world. S/he desperately attempts to gain custody of them. This is done not because of any concern for the children's needs but purely out of a selfish desire to show the world that "these are my offspring and I am a good parent."

When new spouses are present they must be evaluated as well. It is important that these new spouses be available and co-operative. They function as both participants and observers and can be a well of useful information. Sometimes, a new spouse does not wish to be a part of any custody litigation. This in itself is a telling piece of data. These new spouses now play a major role in the household and have the capacity to offer different perceptions of the dynamics within the family. There is no doubt that they may reflect the bias of the person to whom they are married, but they can often provide objective information. The new spouse must investigate his or her feelings regarding instant parenthood, which are valuable in a custody evaluation. A new wife might support her husband in his bid for custody of his children but she may also reveal a reluctance to parent another woman's children. And the opposite may be true; I have seen many cases in which the biological parents were borderline individuals at best and the evaluation was swayed by the presence of a very healthy and competent new stepparent. A very thorough disclosure of marital history combined with personal perceptions of all of the current relationships also offers insight into each individual's capacity to risk, and share information and feelings.

5. Occupational Information. Stability, creativity, initiative, and the ability to meet the challenge of making a living are important factors in determining whether a parent should be awarded custody. Naturally, an evaluator will be more kindly disposed toward the parent who is able to offer a healthy awareness of the world to his or her child. A complete work history of the parent is often a good indication of whether s/he can provide this. Some may feel that this favors the father since many mothers do not have a long history of skill acquisition outside the home, job achievement, or financial security. However, a woman with no previous work experience can still offer her child a solid set of goals, ideals, expected experiences, and desires for the future, as well as a basic awareness of and philosophy regarding work and finances. For such women, the questions concerning employment have to be altered so that these data can be elicited. The mother needs to show that she is aware of the adjustments she will have to make after the dissolution of her marriage. She must understand how the changes in her lifestyle will affect her financial status. If she is to provide financially for her child, she might have to seek further academic or vocational education, which can be costly. She needs to think these problems through thoroughly in order that her understanding be clearly communicated in the psychological evaluation.

6. Education. This is designed not only to get an idea of how much education the parent has, but also to demonstrate the individual's values with regard to education. This is basically an open-ended section and additional questions should be asked to evaluate the individual's concept of his or her own educational needs as well as those of the child. Having an elaborate education is not a prerequisite for being a good parent, but caring about your child's educational needs is a worthwhile value to bring to light.

7. Relationship with the Child. This part of the interview deals with how much the parent really knows about the child and what they can or do share together. A substantial amount of time should be spent on this section in order to find out how the parent views the child as a person. Some of the questions are highly specific and others are open-ended, offering the parent an opportunity to expound on the quality of his or her relationship with the child. The questions are designed to demonstrate the parent's qualities of caring and awareness of the child's needs. In addition, further insight can be gained into how well the parent may be capable of meeting those needs. The parent must have a basic knowledge of his or her child, and a realistic assessment of the child's intellectual, social, and educational abilities and shortcomings. The parent must demonstrate motivation to meet his or her child's needs as well as the intellectual and social resources relevant to the ability to be an effective parent.

8. Additional Information. The DTACC Structured Interview is by no means complete. It would be unrealistic to expect that a single structured examination could ask every question or bring out everything the parent wishes to say. The clinician will want to ask follow-up questions. S/he may wish to know about daily habits such as smoking or drug or alcohol use. Useful data may come from inquiring about a parent's experiences with his or her own parents. This often sheds a great deal of light on what sort of parenting model this person was exposed to as a child.

This section also offers the parent the opportunity to talk about special areas not covered in the interview, and the psychologist should delve into other uncovered areas at this time. Frequently a parent will bring letters of reference from friends and neighbors testifying to good character and fitness as a parent. These letters are usually worthless, since they are obviously biased accounts by people who have no familiarity with the true family dynamics. I would advise the parent to let the psychologist know that these letters exist, but not to bring them or insist that they be considered as evidence of good character. Parents have also been known to bring pictures of their home, their child at his or her last birthday party, the family dog, or the Rolls Royce. It has been my policy to permit parents to show me such material since I recognize that this is important to them. Parents should feel that they have had a full opportunity to be heard. Furthermore, these materials may have some small value, but often this "evidence" is barely credible and will not be included in the report to the court. All parents have good days with their children and even the worst of parents can produce smiling pictures at Disneyland and letters from well-meaning but ignorant friends and neighbors. Such data are always taken with a large grain of salt.

   9. General Descriptions. This descriptive checklist is a special adjunct to the DTACC Structured Interview. It is essentially a mental status examination and concerns those variables most necessary for determining whether a positive and productive relationship can exist between parent and child. It is important for the parent to be aware of the fact that s/he is being evaluated and judged on numerous psychologocial criteria during the interview. This checklist is valuable when the clinician is writing the actual report, as it generates a great deal of information that can be translated into descriptive statements. It also helps to clearly identify the parent in the evaluator's memory as s/he reviews all the data.

   When parents come for a custody evaluation they should be prepared to offer as much information as the evaluator requires to make an effective decision. This data will be reflected in the report to the court; parents should expect to see a liberal sprinking of direct quotes from their session with the evaluator in the report to the court. Additional test information will also be incorporated, but the DTACC Structured Interview, which is one example of an evaluative interview, covers specific and general areas of data that are most often presented to and carefully studied by the judge.

Other Tests. One response does not a test make, and one test does not an evaluation make. A thorough evaluation for custody cannot consist of an interview alone no matter how comprehensive it might be. Psychologists are clearly differentiated from their psychiatric brethren because psychologists have special skills in gathering information through the use of tests. Unlike psychiatrists, psychologists are specifically licensed to administer and interpret tests. Because graduate schools have been de-emphasizing this area in recent years, many psychologists are poorly prepared to correctly utilize the wide range of available psychometric or assessment techniques. Other psychologists, in an effort to join the psychiatric ranks, have completely disowned or forsaken their testing skills. These psychologoists will often be seen in court ranting about how poor tests are and how the average layman can make better predictions than test data can. Some studies have demonstrated this to be true; others have not. My own belief is that testing is a very valuable adjunct in custody decision-making. A conscientious and well-trained psychologist should have a large arsenal of testing techniques available. A parent undergoing an evaluation should expect to take tests so that the evaluator can see that person from different perspectives. It is my opinion that an evaluation which does not include any formal objective testing is not only incomplete, but incompetent.

Many will argue that psychological tests are not as standardized as we are led to believe; that they aren't as statistically valid or reliable as they purport to be. The psychological literature is as replete with attempts to devalue the use of tests as it is with studies that support it. The psychiatric interview, on the other hand, has no statistical reliability or validity. It can not be effectively measured, quantified, or replicated with significant statistical accuracy. Therefore, it is my opinion that more objective psychological tests have a valid place in the custody evaluation.

Of the thousands of psychological tests available, some have very specific relevance to a custody or visitation case. Clinicians will no doubt use their favorite test or combination of tests. My preferences are for the Minnesota Multiphasic Personality Inventory, the Sentence Completion Test, the Rorschach Technique, and the Symptom Checklist in combination with the DTACC Structured Interview. With the exception of the Rorschach and the Structured Interview, these tests can be administered to the parent without a psychologist present. The self-administered tests can be taken at home, in an adjoining testing room in the psychologist's office, or on an office computer.

The scoresheet of the Minnesota Multiphasic Personality Inventory (M.M.P.I.) may be sent to one of many well-respected computer interpretation services or scored by hand using official templates supplied by the company. The actuarial services offer the clinician a thorough print-out report covering the basic scales as well as many of the lesser used or research scales. My own preference is for self-scoring, which produces a more clinical rather than an actuarial evaluation. A clinical interpretation done by the examining psychologist will take into account the special relationships between and among scales. Scoring of this test is statistical and objective but the interpretation is highly subjective and certainly dependent on the skill and diagnostic experience of the psychologist.

The M.M.P.I. presents a wealth of data. The parent's ability and willingness to present honest information is noted on the validity scales. There are three of these scales which allow us to know if the individual is defensive or trying to lie, fake good, or fake bad. In order to successfully interpret the protocol, the validity scales must fall within the statistical range that indicates that the M.M.P.I. accurately represents the individual's current personality characteristics. Once this criterion is satisfied, the remainder of the scales can be interpreted. The current version of the M.M.P.I. measures fourteen specific and numerous less specific personality areas. It can be interpreted in many ways by different clinicians with different orientations and techniques. A general description of the scales can be found in many sources that are specific to M.M.P.I. research. At this writing the M.M.P.I. is undergoing a significant revision. The M.M.P.I.-2 will have more content scales which will offer further data.

The Minnesota Multiphasic Personality Inventory has been a rich area of study over the years. It is always being updated with a view to understanding various populations of people. In describing this test I will present a broad and superficial description of the scales without being overly technical. Transcribing the raw scores into statistical values reveals a profile demonstrating the qualitative aspect of each scale. The placement of an individual's scores on this profile indicates different areas of potential psychopathology. The HS (hypochondriasis) scale tests whether the individual internalizes anxiety into various hypochondriacal and psychosomatic disturbances. It reveals how the individual is in touch with him- or herself as a physical person and how s/he handles the placement of anxiety in his or her body. Scale D (depression) reflects levels of the internalization of anxiety into various modes of depressive functioning. HY (hysteria) deals with a wide range of characteristics, measuring hysteria, hystrionic behavior under stress, the level of anxiety created from within, as well as rigidity versus flexibility in thinking. HS, D, and HY are often viewed as the neurotic end of the continuum, and their relative positions in relation to each other are most important in the interpretations.

Scale PD (psychopathic deviate) illustrates the gamut of psychopathy. It also may reflect an individual's manipulative skills, organization, planning abilities, initiative, intellect, and creativity. Although societal values would have us view manipulation as a negative concept or trait, it can be seen positively, as for a competent and effective individual to have the ability to structure his or her environment. We all desire to have our needs met, and this scale permits insight into how the individual accomplishes this process.

The MF (masculinity-femininity) scale reveals data regarding an individual's sexual identification, the extent of traditional role orientation, psychosexual pathology, and the expression of feelings of warmth, tenderness, and closeness. In addition, an individual can be measured as regards passivity versus assertiveness. This scale can also present data on esthetic orientation, philosophical positions, and one's ability to relate to someone of the opposite sex.

The PA (paranoia) scale covers a wide range of data. It can reveal personality traits ranging from extreme gullibility at one end of the continuum to the possibility of an active paranoid delusional system on the other. This scale may also offer significant data regarding the individual's sensitivity to personal needs as well as his or her awareness of the needs and motives of others.

PT (psychasthenia) indicates the level of tension and anxiety, while the neighboring scale, SC (schizophrenia), reveals information regarding external stressors, psychotic thought processes, and the possibility of hallucinations, delusions, or primary thought process disturbances.

The MA (hypomania) scale is interpreted in a multitude of ways. Some see it as a measure of emotional energy available to the individual, while others view this scale as an indicator of efficiency and intellectual skills. It is used to test an individual's capacity to accept new challenges in the environment as well as utilize native initiative and creativity. When this is exaggerated, the scale can also demonstrate rebelliousness, alienation from others, and destructiveness in personal relationships.

The final traditional scale, SI (social introversion) reflects the individual's attitude regarding important close interpersonal relationships. It measures introversion-extroversion, the ability to deal effectively with groups and individuals, risking skills, sharing of feelings, and interpersonal sophistication. There are literally hundreds of minor scales which are in continuous use. Four new scales were recently added to the test profile that reflect anxiety, repression, ego strength, and addictive tendencies.

All of the M.M.P.I. scales in various combinations reveal the individual's emotional and personality strengths and weaknesses. This test, like all tests, is not infallible, but is well worth administering since it is highly informative. The M.M.P.I. measures pathology in many areas and offers a rapid estimate of emotional well-being or emotional disturbance. The psychologist has to assess how much energy the parent has to offer the child, how the parent operates under stress with regard to thought organization, whether the individual internalizes anxiety into neurotic symptomatology, etc. The more data we can generate, the faster the pieces of the custody puzzle will fall into place.

Sentence completion tests can be administered in a number of different forms. There are many well-recognized tests from which to choose, most of which offer alternative versions for males and females, adults and children. Any one of these may be utilized, and tend to yield a documentation of needs, skills, insights, judgments, general life values, social awareness, relationship skills, and problem-solving techniques. In addition, a sentence completion inventory can be used to obtain representative samples of handwriting, spelling, grammar, and general communication skills.

A checklist of physiological and psychological symptoms is valuable in getting a quick idea of the parent's self-awareness, physiological concerns, and potential neurotic disabilities. The subject is asked to respond to a straightforward checklist on which s/he rates about sixty physical and emotional discomforts. S/he is asked how much these symptoms bother him or her, and must rate them on a scale from "not bothered at all" to "extremely concerned." Although this is a very easy test for the subject to manipulate, in my experience, people will freely admit to the symptoms listed that apply to them.

The Rorschach Technique (popularly known as the Ink Blot Test) is one of the most widely used and most widely debated psychological tests. The literature cites hundreds of studies both pro and con with regard to the statistical reliability, validity, and usefulness of the Rorschach. Whether a clinician selects this test or some other measure of projection (such as the Thematic Apperception Test) seems to depend solely on that person's graduate school education and those parts of the psychological research literature s/he chooses to accept. It has been my experience that the Rorschach Technique gives a good estimate of how a patient structures ambiguous stimuli (and, by extension, an ambiguous world) and how s/he utilizes emotional affect, intelligence, and awareness. It can also yield information about bizarre or inappropriate ideation which the clinician may wish to follow-up with other tests or more questions.

The Rorschach Technique can be an invaluable assessment technique for evaluating both adults and children, but its success is largely dependent on the skill and experience of the clinician. Some psychologists use a standard "cookbook" or actuarial approach while others interpret the Rorschach Technique in a more traditional psychoanalytic fashion. Between these two there are many other interpretive approaches. The parent's perception of detail, position, form, structure, movement, texture, color, and content are but a few of the determinants studied. These reveal much about whether this parent may be expected to present an orderly conception of the world and a competent value system to the child. These perceptions are discussed in the report of the custody evaluation to ensure that the court has a thorough insight into the qualitative aspects of the personality and parenting skills of each individual evaluated.

With regard to the testing procedures, we must be completely honest in recognizing that the psychological aspect of the custody evaluation is a very contrived and artificial situation. In a few small hours the evaluator has to make numerous judgments and determinations that will affect many lives. Clients must be dealt with who only present their best sides. Any aspects of their personalities which may be detrimental to their causes will be left at home. Perhaps the only honest way to conduct a custody evaluation is to move in with the family for a month and live with them. At the end of this time an evaluator would probably be far more certain which parent would be the best custodian. Of course, this is highly impractical. Because of this, psychologists have to maximize the brief opportunity they have with each family by using specific psychological instruments carefully selected to uncover the most important information. This type of evaluation should not always be composed of a standard battery, but should utilize some core tests with which the evaluator is expert. The psychologist should also tailor the testing to the needs of the client. For example, in a situation in which a parent has been confined to a mental hospital for a considerable period of time and is now appealing aggressively to the court to get visitation rights, far more complete testing must be done. One rule of thumb in a psychological evaluation is to use whatever one must in order to generate the most data and to develop these data into a thorough and comprehensive report. The court appreciates a complete technical study. Because of this, it is vital that parents agree to cooperate with the testing procedures.

DTACC Structured Interview-Children

Date _____

Name _____ Age _____

Birthdate _____ Birthplace _____

Current Address _____

_____

Now living with: _____

_____

Current Issue

Do you understand why you are here today and what we will be doing? If so, please explain it to me so that we will both understand and be thinking the same thing. If not, I would like you to understand that everyone in your family loves you very much. Even though your mother and father have decided that they do not wish to be married and cannot live together anymore, they both want to make sure that your life is comfortable and happy. We are here today so that I can get more information from everyone about how they feel and what they want. I also want to understand you as well as I can so that I will be able to help the judge decide what will be best for you and for your parents, too. Do you understand that? . . . This will be your big chance to let me know all of the things that are important to you, all about how you feel and what kinds of things you think about. After we meet, I will write a long letter to the judge and let him know what you and I feel is important. Your mother has a lawyer who will talk for her in court and your father also has a lawyer who talks for him. My job is to talk for you, so I will be like your lawyer. (If the child is verbal, s/he must understand these concepts before proceeding through the DTACC Structured Interview.)

School

1. What school are you attending now?

2. What grade are you in?

3. What is your teacher's name?

4. What subjects do you like most in school?

5. Why do you like these subjects?

6. What subjects do you not like in school?

7. Why don't you like these subjects?

8. What were your grades on your last report card?

9. How do you feel about your teacher and why?

10. Do you enjoy going to school in the morning?

11. How do you get to school?

12. What do you do when you come home from school? Tell me what your usual day is like, and what your schedule is like at home.

Friends and Siblings

1. Do you have good friends at school (the kind you can tell secrets to)?

2. Tell me about them and what you do with them.

3. Do you have friends at home in the neighborhood? Tell me about them and what you do with them.

4. How often do you see your friends?

5. Do you ever have anyone sleeping over?

6. Do you ever sleep at their homes?

7. Do you enjoy these sleep-overs?

8. Tell me the names of your brothers and sisters, if any?

9. How old are they?

10. Who starts most of the fights?

11. Who wins the fights?

12. How do you get along with your brothers and sisters?

13. Which one do you spend the most time with?

14. What do you do together?

15. How do they get along with your parents?

16. Have you talked with your brothers and sisters about the problems we are trying to get information about today?

17. What do your brothers and sisters think should be done?

18. Why do you think they feel this way?

19. Do you agree with them?

20. Tell me about your thoughts and ideas.

21. Tell me about your brothers's and sisters's friends.

22. What do they do together?

23. Do you ever do things with them too?

24. What kinds of play activities do you all do together?

25. Do your parents have close friends?

26. Tell me about them.

27. What kinds of things have they done together?

28. Who is your favorite friend in all the world and why?

_____

Parents

1. Mother's name and age.

2. How do you get along with your mother?

3. What activities do you do with her?

4. Tell me all the things you like most about your mother.

5. What don't you like about her?

6. How would you like her to change these things?

7. Is she ever involved in your school activities?

8. What things does she do?

9. Does she ever help you with homework or projects?

10. Does she do a good job helping with homework?

11. Explain how she helps.

12. Do your brothers and sisters get along with your mother?

13. Who gets along with her best and why?

14. Does she have another job beside her work at home?

15. What does she do?

16. Do you think she likes her job? Why?

17. What does your mother do best of all in the whole world?

18. What does she do for you that is very special?

19. What is there that you would like her to do for you that she either does not want to or is not able to?

20. Is she a good cook?

21. What does she cook best?

22. Do you think that your mother loves you?

23. How do you know?

---

1. Father's name and age.

2. How do you get along with your father?

3. What activities do you do with him?

4. Tell me all the things you like most about your father.

5. What don't you like about him?

6. How would you like him to change these things?

7. Is he ever involved in your school activities?

8. What things does he do?

9. Does he ever help you with homework or projects?

10. Does he do a good job helping with homework?

11. Explain how he helps.

12. Do your brothers and sisters get along with your father?

13. Who gets along with him best and why?

14. Does he have a job outside your home?

15. What does he do?

16. Do you think that he likes his job? Why?

17. What does your father do best of all in the whole world?

18. What does he do for you that is very special?

19. What is there that you would like him to do for or with you that he either does not want to or is not able to do?

20. Is he a good cook?

21. What does he cook best?

22. Do you think that your father loves you?

23. How do you know?

Current Situation

1. Which parent do you live with right now?

2. How long has it been this way?

3. How often do you visit your (noncustodial parent)?

4. What do you do on these visits?

5. Do your bothers and sisters go with you?

6. How do you feel about this schedule?

7. How do your brothers and sisters feel about it?

8. In what way do your brothers and sisters think this schedule should be changed?

9. If you were the judge, would you change the way things are going now?

10. How would you change it, and why?

11. What ideas do you have that you would like me to tell the judge?

Stepparent or Live-in "Parent"
(If mother is remarried or has a "significant other.")

1. I want you to tell me about (use name). Do you like him?

2. Why do you feel this way?

3. What do the two of you do together?

4. Do you enjoy talking with him?

5. What do you talk about?

6. How do you think he feels about you?

7. How do you know?

8. Does he have any other children?

9. What are their names and ages?

10. Do you see them often?

11. How do you get along with them?

12. What do you do together?

(If father is remarried or has a "significant other.")

1. I want you to tell me about (use name). Do you like her?

2. Why do you feel this way?

3. What do the two of you do together?

4. Do you enjoy talking with her?

5. What do you talk about?

6. How do you think she feels about you?

7. How do you know?

8. Does she have any other children?

9. What are their names and ages?

10. Do you see them often?

11. How do you get along with them?

12. What do you do together?

Wishes

1. If you could have any three wishes in the world (except more wishes), what would they be?

2. What animal would you like to be and why?

3. Describe your favorite meal.

Descriptions of Child

General physical appearance and hygiene.

Facial expression.

Range of emotion.

General affect.

Cooperativeness.

Speech.

Clarity of thought.

Manipulation.

Social skills.

Body movements.

Humor, sarcasm.

Intellect.

Insight level.

Judgment level.

Orientation (three spheres).

Information recall.

Small-detail awareness.

Compulsiveness.

Planning skills.

Creativity.

Small-muscle skills.

Large-muscle skills.

Imagination.

Anger at parents, stepparents.

Consistency.

Ability to express feelings.

Sensitivity to own needs.

Sensitivity to needs of others.

Awareness of custody issue.

Sex-role assignment.

Truth-telling.

Test cooperation.

Independence.

Activity level.

Affection skills.

General self-image.

Acceptance of others.

Personal depth.

Hand preference.

Foot preference.

Eye preference.

Eye tracking.

Eye accommodation.

Gait.

Evaluating the Child: The Use of the DTACC Structured Interview and Other Tests

Just as the DTACC Structured Interview for adults is not designed as a questionnaire, neither is the interview for children. Children should always be seen in a face-to-face situation and should not be evaluated through the use of fill-in tests. The DTACC is an example of an interview process which can be utilized by a psychologist to collect information in a structured and comprehensive fashion. It cannot ever be used in a rigid or formal manner since children are often more comfortable in an interview which permits them to skip around from one area to another. Most evaluators will find that with a friendly, caring, and calm approach, they will be able to obtain answers to all of the questions as well as collect additional information outside the interview format.

Just like the adult interview, the children's interview covers nine areas:

1. General Information. This is an identification section simply to help the examiner establish basic information about where each child resides and how old each child is at the time of the testing. It sets the stage for the upcoming questions.

2. Current Issue. Frequently, children are not prepared for the testing by their parents or have been misinformed about it. They often have no idea why they are in the office. They may have some idea of the purpose of the evaluation but may still be confused. Prior to the evaluation, the parent ideally should prepare the child. This preparation should not include specific instructions as to what the child should say but offer general notions of what will be done. The parent should discuss with the examiner what is expected of the child, then give the child an overview of the purpose and structure of the evaluation. The evaluator, too, must tell the child about the evaluation's basic structure as well as explain why it must be undertaken. Even if the child understands, it is wise for the examiner to restate the issue so that a basic rapport is established. The child is usually substantially relieved by this, and eager to cooperate because s/he understands that s/he is being given a voice in determining the direction of his or her life.

3. School. School performance serves as a reliable yardstick of the child's emotional health. Very bright children under unusual amounts of situational stress may be experiencing difficulty in learning. This is often the first place anxiety manifests itself. More chronic anxiety may produce evidence of long-term failure in school. The child's feelings should be checked out carefully with regard to learning skills, the learning environment, subjects with which the child experiences difficulty, and subjects in which the child does well.

Relationships with teachers can reveal evidence of the child's ability to interact with adults and authority figures. If the child perceives that s/he is not doing well with his or her teachers, a release of information should be requested from the parents so that the evaluator can verify these perceptions with school personnel. Most teachers and principals are happy to cooperate if the proper school records release is provided. Consultation with the psychologist can help them deal with the child's anxiety, which is often a result of the crumbling home environment.

Questions in this section also elicit information about the kind of educational climate the child is offered by the parents. Questions dealing with the normal school and home routines can provide very useful data. A parent who chooses to foster a climate conducive to learning may have more insight into a child's needs, abilities, and potential achievement. These are significant areas, since most evaluators look for some assurance that the parents know the value of an education in preparing their children for the world.

4. Friends, Siblings. All relationships, both familial and interpersonal, must be thoroughly studied. If the child feels alienated from peers and siblings, this may cause anxiety, dissatisfaction, and fearfulness. It is critical to find out how "connected" children feel to their current home and school environments, and this is accomplished by questioning both peer and sibling relationships. It is useful for the examiner to cross-check these answers with those of each sibling to correctly assess each child's view of the truth, since children often attempt to protect their families by distorting the truth. The evaluator looks for information about the children's ability to make friends and share close personal experiences with others, including parents.

Children also can supply information about their parents' ability to relate to other adults as well as to their own relatives. Parents who are unable to establish close ties with others may have some specific interpersonal difficulties, which in turn can be highly detrimental to their children, since parents with such problems do not make healthy role models. The family unit is not an island unto itself, but exists in a world busy with personal interactions.

5. Parents. Of course, the main thrust of the interview with the children is to investigate the nature of their relationship to their individual parents. This is done by closely scrutinizing: 1) activities which are shared; 2) the children's likes and; 3) dislikes; 4) closeness with parents; 5) the manner in which the parents help the children with everyday experiences; 6) how the parents model behavior for the children; 7) how the children experience their parents' love. Questions are asked regarding both the mother and father, as well as stepparents, boyfriends, girlfriends, and live-ins. The bulk of the interview should be spent on this section, since the evaluator needs to glean as much information as possible regarding interaction between parent and child. Again, the DTACC Structured Interview is often just a starting point for more spontaneous, detailed questions.

6. **Current Situation.** Children rarely ever see issues of custody and visitation the same way that parents see them. Children view the experience from an emotional as well as an objective point of view. They view the behavior of their parents and quickly size them up, realizing how they are manipulating their children and how in turn they can manipulate their parents. Children gauge how hysterical, angry, and irrational their parents tend to get with each other, which gives the children a great deal of power in many situations.

Each child is a primary source of input in any custody case. This section of the interview gives children a direct opportunity to discuss the needs to be communicated to the court. The examiner should *not* directly ask any child where s/he wants to live. The DTACC Structured Interview does not ask this question, although children are asked in an obtuse manner how the home should be structured. Children are asked about preferences among siblings, whether they agree or disagree with their positions, as well as how the parents should change. These questions reveal much data and are far more productive than asking children directly where they want to live. Most children will not express a direct preference for fear of alienating the noncustodial parent. However, some will spontaneously state a preference for one parent and when this happens, it should be followed through in depth.

It is never wise for a parent to directly pressure a child. The effects of this type of pressure are difficult to assess but its presence becomes obvious in an interview. Many parents will accuse their ex-spouses of attempting to "brainwash" or "poison the child's mind against me." Such language is usually a clue that such situations do exist. The statements of children in this situation should be carefully noted to detect any echoes of parental pressure. A parent may unconsciously program language into a child that reflect a negative opinion of the other spouse. When a five-year-old says that Mother is a "slut," it is a safe bet that this is really the father talking through the child. When a five-year-old discusses the fact that Father is "always late with the support check," it can be safely assumed that s/he is really parroting the mother's statements. Since this section of the psychological inteview gives children ample opportunity to openly discuss feelings about their parents, it should become patently obvious if either parent is attempting to program them.

7. Stepparents. In a large percentage of custody cases we find that stepparents have been part of the children's lives for a considerable time. Stepparents play an interesting, sometimes integral, role in custody disputes. It's not unusual to find out that it was they who forced the entire custody issue in the first place. Often a stepparent sues for custody in order to strip the ex-spouse of all vestiges of the former marriage. The stepparent may be a very strong, loving, and supportive person. When such people are part of the child's life, they should all be thoroughly evaluated, as they are part of the main cast of characters.

8. Fantasy Productions. These questions frequently provide fascinating answers. Fearful children have difficulty creating fantasies. Children who are open, secure, and free from anxiety frequently produce revealing, exciting, and original fantasies. By asking about them, we are given insight into their freedom and flexibility of thought as well as imagination. Almost always, children offer as one of their three wishes a desire that their parents will get back together. This takes place frequently even if both parents have remarried. Asking about fantasies can also provide information regarding the children's reality testing and the depth of the pain created by the dissolution of the parents' marriage.

Other wishes usually reflect affectional needs expressed through a desire for games, food, or special activities. Whether children are able to express their fantasies or not provides a very direct clue to their comfort level and ability to think in a non-anxious and flexible fashion. I recently interviewed a four-year-old boy who, when asked for his wishes, beamed broadly and said, "What I want is all the chocolatey-chipped cookies in the whole world." He relished the opportunity to express this secret wish out loud and accentuated it with a devilish chuckle to indicate how pleased he was with himself. This was a good indication of the child's affective skills, his ability to be broad and expansive in thinking and openly share his private feelings. It also might have indicated his need for affection through an emotional tie-in between food and love.

9. General Descriptions. As with the adult version of the DTACC Structured Interview, the children's version also has a descriptive checklist. The examiner should fill this out immediately after the interview session. It only takes a few moments of the evaluator's time and requires just a few descriptive words for each concept. This is an excellent way to generate statements for the report as well as providing a general overview of the subject's behavior. It can be easily used to identify the children and gives a broad picture of the specific variables that enter into judgments regarding custody.

Children in these intensive interview sessions frequently will retreat and attempt to hide behind the phrase, "I don't know." If the evaluator allows them to establish a "response set" whereby they are permitted to use this evasive phrase time after time and get away with not responding, it can very easily defeat the entire process. Although I am not by nature or philosophy a behaviorist, it is my strong opinion that a behavioral ploy can be used very effectively to circumvent such a response. I utilize a roll of pennies which is emptied into a small plastic pail and given to the child. No explanation is offered for this action; the child is simply told that s/he may have whatever money is "left over." Each time the child says that s/he does not know, the examiner reaches over and quietly plucks one penny from the child's pail, places it in the examiner's own little pail, and repeats the question. Even though no explanation is given, the child very quickly gains insight into what is happening and rapidly shelves the "I don't know" response. This is also a very handy technique to use in psychotherapy with a young child. After the first session the child may have only ten of the original fifty cents remaining, but after the second session s/he usually will have at least forty-five. Once a child learns to be forthcoming, this procedure can be abandoned.

At the end of the testing session, most psychologists will offer a child a small reward for his or her work and cooperation. Frequently, these evaluations will be repeated within six months or a year, sometimes longer. The child usually has very positive feelings about return visits if s/he has been positively reinforced after the first session. Sweets are a poor reinforcer, in addition to not being very healthy, so rewards should take other forms. I offer children two small rubber animals which they can select from a large box of approximately three hundred different ones. They enjoy this selection process as much as the actual reinforcement.

Other Tests. It is good practice when evaluating children in custody cases to view them from many different perspectives. In addition to the DTACC Structured Interview, it is necessary to assess how reliable their perceptions are in this time of stress and crisis. For this reason, I always utilize an intelligence test. The intellectual level of children has a definite bearing on how insightful, creative, and aware they are about their own needs as well as those of their parents. The Peabody Picture Vocabulary

Test gives a rapid estimate of a child's sight vocabulary. It can be administered to the very youngest of children as all they have to do is point to a picture that correctly identifies a word. It can also be used with teens. The revised Peabody gives the children's standard score equivalent, stanine, the percentile in which they fall with regard to their own age group, and the current mental age. The mental age is then compared to the current chronological age in order to see at what level the children are actually functioning. Often, when a very young child has a mental age of a child much older (which suggests excellent verbal and intellectual skills) this indicates whether the child can communicate effectively with the judge in chambers.

Once we have measured intelligence, we need a rapid measure of organic integrity. The Bender Visual-Motor Gestalt test offers a gross measure of organicity. Children are offered structured geometric forms on small cards and must simply translate these visual stimuli into motoric responses as they reproduce the figures on one side of a single piece of paper. It is not highly sensitive for very young children but can usually be counted on to alert an examiner to the presence of brain pathology. Such findings are dependent on the examiner's expertise. The Bender test also permits the evaluator to measure eye-tracking skills (helpful in evaluating learning disabilities), planning and organization skills, and general and specific visual-motor ability and perception.

Cognitive testing should be followed by projective testing to reveal possible problems with the children's emotional health. The projective drawings of houses, trees, and people offer data about current familial and interpersonal struggles, self-image experiences, and identification with peers. The kinetic family drawing (the children are asked to draw a family doing something) can reveal a great deal of information. It can offer insights into the children's specific familial experiences and thoughts. Although children are told to draw a family rather than their family, they will invariably render a scene specific to their own family life. We can often see which parent they identify with and the quality and depth of their interaction. Often children will draw a family engaged in parallel rather than interactional activity, with the favored parent shown as being more aware, interested, and considerate of their needs.

The Rorschach Technique or "ink blot test" is the old standby projective test to assess intrapsychic dynamics. Children's responses to the Rorschach blots reveal the extent of stress in their environment as well as their ability to cope with these struggles. As mentioned previously, the Rorschach is disputed as a valid statistical test. However, it clearly stimulates children and supplies valuable information which can be evaluated subjectively, if not objectively. Children enjoy taking the Rorschach, as it gives them an opportunity to be relaxed and to play the game of offering a structure to an ambiguous environment. They especially enjoy the fact that there are no right or wrong answers, that they can turn the cards any way they wish, and that they can allow themselves to be creative, original, and use their best imagination.

To summarize this section, it is critical to gather as much data from the children as possible. A suggested method for doing this is: 1) a thorough review of the custody situation through the use of the DTACC Structured Interview or a similar instrument; 2) a measure of intelligence; 3) a measure of possible organic disability; and 4) the use of projective tests to get at the children's internal projections, feelings, and needs. This represents the characteristics of an evaluation aimed at collecting enough data to assist the court in making this life-changing decision. This type of evaluation may require many hours, depending on the cooperation and abilities of each child. No matter how long it takes it should be accomplished as much in depth as is possible.

Evaluating Children and Parents Together: Pros and Cons

A professional and competent custody evaluation may take many forms, and there is certainly no single prescribed method for accomplishing it. Clinicians will utilize their own styles, backgrounds, skills, experiences, and successful techniques. Some specifically enjoy testing children and spend the bulk of their time dealing with information they elicit through psychological tests and play techniques. Others feel that the main thrust of a study should be on parenting skills and will therefore concentrate their time on the parents, performing a more cursory examination of the children. Many psychologists prefer not to examine very young children at all.

A popular evaluation style is to work in a team with another clinician. One evaluator will see the parents and another will test the children. The data is then pooled and the final report will be drawn as a collaboration between the two psychologists. There are obvious difficulties inherent in this approach unless both evaluators have similar philosophical leanings as well as similar training and experiences. I have found this approach to be highly beneficial, though, since it involves two professionals who can verify each other's perceptions. This approach works best when one of the evaluators is clearly designated the team leader and takes the major responsibility for coordinating the data and writing the report.

There is another method which has gained a great deal of popularity over the years. This involves evaluating the child in the presence of each parent. Some clinicians feel that this is the only accurate method for judging the relationship between parent and child. They further contend that only in this way can the parenting skills of the adults be correctly assessed. A clinician must have a large, elaborate, and well-stocked playroom in order to put this philosophical position into practice. The theoretical stance espoused by these practitioners is that they place the adult in the child's world. The adult who has been introduced to the playroom must function with the child in a cooperative manner and can thus be observed. The psychologist watches the child and parent at play and records the behavioral data gathered from this. This can be done through the use of a one-way mirror, or with the evaluator observing from outside of the designated playing space. The interaction can be recorded using video or audio equipment, or through very complete note-taking.

Once in the playroom, the child will either go from toy to toy or quickly settle on one. The parent and child may attempt to engage each other or may play at parallel activities. Most parents spend the bulk of this type of play session doting on the child's every action. They try very hard to pretend that the evaluator is not present and not observing. The child usually does not care about being observed, but in most cases, the parent never forgets.

What data can be gained by using the procedure of play observation between parent and child? My opinion is that it offers very little information pertinent to a custody evaluation. Of course, if a parent should lose control of his or her temper and begin suddenly to beat the child in front of the evaluator, this will be significant data. But the child is usually so absorbed in play that the presence of the parent means very little. And it has been my experience that almost any parent and any child can sustain an hour of play even if their basic relationship is extremely poor.

For example, in a recent evaluation, a psychologist commented that the relationship between a father and his son was cooperative, loving, and generally warm. What the psychologist did not know was the child had told another psychologist that he hated his father and never wanted to see him again. The playroom psychologist was unaware that the father had abducted the child six months earlier and taken him out of the country. The boy was returned to the mother after many months and only after coordinating the services of a number of international police agencies. This experience had been enormously traumatic for the young child, who had refused to visit his father since his return, and was experiencing disturbing nightmares each evening as well as acting out traumatic episodes in preschool. Although he was only four years old, this child was quite verbal about expressing his fear of his father, although he would express this only when not in his father's immediate presence. In addition, a few minutes prior to the playroom session with the child, the father came to the office and greeted him with a large stuffed animal. Any person, psychologist or not, observing the father and son playing would surely be deceived as to the boy's real feelings toward his father, and the father's awareness of the boy's needs. We are all familiar with how the victims of aggression will try to appease their aggressor. The child who has had his or her integrity assailed constantly will try hard to placate an abusing parent. The child may come back frequently for more abuse, with this vicious pattern continuing unabated until adulthood. So what we see in the playroom session might be a well-programmed act by both parent and child.

What are the most effective procedures and methods for these family custody evaluations? I do not presume to know the best of all possible procedures. However, most evaluators agree that there are some particularly efficient processes that can be utilized. I began my studies when there were no other evaluators to trade information and techniques with, and so have evolved my own experiences over the years into an efficient approach that seems to elicit the most important information. My preference is first to see each parent individually. I utilize the DTACC Structured Interview for a comprehensive session and then may administer the Rorschach Technique. The parent is then taken to a well-lit private testing office where coffee and tea are available, and smoking is permitted. In these relaxed environs, the parent completes the Minnesota Multiphasic Personality Inventory (all 567 questions, and not the "short form" of four hundred questions). A sentence completion test and symptom checklist are also administered. There are no time limits on these tests and the parent is encouraged to take as much time as needed to complete the tests. Parents are also urged to write down anything they may have forgotten during the initial interview that they feel has importance for the question of custody. Frequently some of the data tapped in the tests will reveal information parents feel is very significant and must be communicated. Even though these tests are self-administered and there are validity checks in the scoring, I prefer that they not be taken home by parents.

After testing both parents, the data is studied to look for any discrepancies between their stories and their individual perceptions. Then the court documents, declarations, and any materials supplied by the parents or attorneys are studied. If there are still unanswered questions or severe discrepancies between their positions, the parent or parents are again interviewed individually to follow these up and clarify the issues. After all of these data are collected, the child is brought in for a thorough evaluation. The DTACC Structured Interview for Children is used, then the Peabody Picture Vocabulary Test, Bender Visual-Motor Gestalt Test, Projective Drawings, and Rorschach Technique are administered. Each child should be evaluated individually, not in the presence of siblings or parents. This yields the purest information, since the child really feels that an unhindered, personal rapport has been established between him- or herself and the examiner.

Very young children (ages two to four), or children who are not highly verbal, should have the opportunity to experience an active play interview. Parents can expect the psychologist to have specific toys on hand for these sessions. I use hand puppets, tiny doll families with furniture, rubber animals, small tools, cowboys and Indians, soldiers, dolls, and a large yellow crane. The crane is quite attractive and gets the child's attention easily, thereby establishing a "play" mind-set. The child is permitted to play alone and only after a few minutes should specific toys and situations be introduced. After a few minutes of play with a doll family, questions may be asked, such as: "Show me what they do at breakfast," "Show me what they all do after dinner," "Show me how the baby is taken care of and who does it best." More complex familial and interpersonal interactions are suggested as the child plays. Seeing how the child manipulates the doll family figures reveals a great deal about the roles in the home. This yields valuable information about the effectiveness of the parents. Handpuppets and "pretend" conversations are also very effective ways of getting data. Children under four are sometimes observed in this type of play session, sometimes not.

A custody evaluation involving infants is the most problematic since all of the data must be elicited from the parents. It is rarely of any value to spend much time with infants.

It is interesting to note the behavior of the children while they are in the waiting room. Some will sit politely while others will show signs of agitated, even violent anxiety. This may be a reflection of the kind of parenting to which they have been exposed. Children should not be left alone in the waiting room, even for a few minutes, as this can be a very frightening experience for them. If both a young child and his or her parents are to be interviewed, I always require that they bring another person to be with the child while the parent is being evaluated. Being left alone in the waiting room may foster negative feelings in the child, so that when the time comes for his or her appointment, s/he can be hostile and resistant.

To summarize, my experience has indicated to me that very little can be learned from observing the parent and child in a play session together. The responsible parent involved in a custody dispute wants all of the pertinent data to come out. The responsible evaluator will collect as much data as possible from each parent individually, and then from each child in the family individually. The playroom parent-child observation, on the other hand, frequently misrepresents the relationship between the two. There is a limit to what an observer can gather without taking a more active involvement. Not long ago, I saw a father and his young daughter playing cards in the halls of the courthouse. Any passerby would have assumed that they had a healthy and happy relationship. I then heard a series of taped telephone conversations between these same two. In these conversations the father was rude, abusive, impatient, continuously used profanity, lost his temper, was manipulative, and showed a total lack of support for the child's needs. These chilling tape recordings were far more representative of their true relationship than that seemingly pleasant card game they were playing on the courthouse bench.

4
The Psychological Report

Style of Presentation

When a custody evaluation is completed, a report is issued to the attorneys, judge, court mediator, and other interested parties. It combines all of the data and should be presented in a cohesive and effective manner. Writing a definitive psychological report is an impossible task. No matter how excellent the report may seem when it is first written, it is very easy to go back through it when it is "cold" and shred it to bits. Every psychologist has had this experience. It is frustrating, even enraging, to look back through one's report and realize that it might not have effectively communicated the point one had intended.

There are as many report writing styles as there are report writers, and surely as many as there are graduate school supervisors. When I was in school, one supervisor told me that he wanted only a *narrative* summary that fully presented the data and could be used as a "reference summary." I developed great expertise at this style after a few months. When I went to my first field placement, however, my supervisor there told me that if she saw one summary statement I would be marched out of Psychology and across the quad to the School of Social Work. This supervisor wanted data, data, and more data. She wanted rows and columns of numbers, subtest scores, ratios, raw scores, scaled scores, stanines, statistical correlations, reliability and validity coefficients, and a table of frequencies if it became necessary. Within a few months I developed great expertise at this style. At my next field placement, my new supervisor questioned the inclusion of all of the data in my report. He wanted a test-by-test, psychoanalytically oriented report with a brief summary to "tie up any loose ends," as well as literature citations for each test interpretation made, and data citations for each summary statement made. Within a few months I developed great expertise at *this* style. My next field supervisor wanted to know what all these citations were doing in my report. She wanted all reports to be one-half page long and take the form of a mental status report without mentioning any tests at all. Again, within a few months I developed great expertise at this style. My next supervisor tossed the half page report in my face and asked how I had the nerve to offer so little after having spent six hours testing a patient. He wanted twenty page reports detailing in depth every specific interaction, test response, and dynamic interpretation.

This is typical of how a psychologist learns to write a report. Every psychologist with a rich and varied clinical background of field experience has had to play the game of pleasing his or her supervisor. Although it is confusing to go through this type of experience, it does help the fledgling report writer since it provides exposure to a number of very different communication styles. Eventually the psychologist evolves his or her own personal style of transmitting data.

The major function of the report is to communicate. It must tell a story about a person or about a family. As with any good story, it must have a beginning, a middle, and an end. It should be clear, concise, technical, and professional, but relatively free of excessive or cumbersome jargon. The most important function of the report is that it address the question asked in the initial referral. The report should end with an answer to that question, whether it is a specific diagnosis, an outline of specific dynamics, a statement about which parent may be best for a child, a specific treatment plan, or that no answer can be found at this particular time. The psychologist has the responsibility to educate those who make the referrals so that they ask reasonable and appropriate questions. S/he then has a responsibility to collect appropriate data. S/he must resolve the question by relying on the raw material and the dynamic interpretations made from these data.

A good psychological report is always written with the reader in mind. A report prepared for another psychologist should be significantly different from one prepared for a judge, parent, attorney, psychiatrist, or probation officer. Custody evaluations require a fairly specific style. The psychologist is not only the test administrator and interpreter, but also serves as history-taker, detective, mediator, and consultant to the court. The report must consider the parents's salient life experiences as well as the specific data from the testing session. It should carefully balance the various elements relevant to the case, including the dynamics, the relationships, and the test results. The report should then culminate with a very specific stance. In the custody matter the judge makes the decision, not the psychologist. However, in the report that is issued to the court, the psychologist can present to the judge direct and strong opinions about what should take place. The psychologist becomes an advocate for that particular opinion.

Some psychologists feel that the report should be just an information statement that offers no specific conclusions. The judge would then be left to use this information as an aid in making the judgments. However, I feel that the reason psychologists undertake this assessment in the first place is to offer a firm decision based on their expertise. There is a responsibility inherent in the very process which dictates that a direct statement and conclusion be made. This philosophy puts the evaluator in an advocacy position, since by taking the side of the child's best interests, s/he may necessarily have to take one parent's side against the other. If the judge disagrees with the position of the psychologist, that of course is his or her right. However, I am very much in favor of the evaluator offering the judge a specific position in order to reinforce the strength of the recommendation and so that the judge has a firm position from which to decide the issue. Since the report is such an important communication, one that will affect many lives, it is important that it be carefully enunciated. What follows here are suggestions, based on extensive personal experience, on how a report should be written.

Prior to getting into the body of the report, a cover sheet outlining and describing the tests is most helpful to the judge. Since the report is not written for trained psychologists, it should describe the tests in layman's terms, what they are designed to measure, and how they are administered. The reader should know what kinds of data the tests yield so that s/he can understand why they were selected. This also aids in communicating with parents and attorneys, since the ground rules for a common language are spelled out. Attorneys should read these descriptions carefully so that they can be knowledgeable and specific about them in court. Although it is vital to communicate with parents and attorneys in their idiom, it is also vital to educate them about the psychological idiom.

In preparing the body of the report, my usual procedure is to report on the parents in the order in which they appeared for the evaluation. Very careful notes are taken during the interview so that all of what each parent says can be reported with integrity. Some evaluators feel more comfortable using a tape recorder, and parents should be prepared for this. Sometimes the presence of audio and video equipment can inhibit a parent, which is why handwritten notes are sometimes preferable. In addition, a good shorthand technique will protect the confidentiality of the file.

Reporting all of the parents' statements is important since the evaluator does not have the right to delete any specific area which parents feel has great importance to the case. The information they wish to have communicated to the judge should be conveyed in depth.

The last part of the report is reserved for information and data about the child. This is also thoroughly explicated, both in terms of the behavioral observations and analyses of the test data. The very end of the report should be a thorough summary and include the evaluator's specific recommendations. The summary should be a brief synopsis of the major issues and point out any differences between the parents. The recommendations should be made up of specific conclusions based on the data. As indicated, it is my feeling that the psychologist should submit some very specific recommendations.

Prior to the evaluation, the parents are asked to sign a release form. This permits copies of the report to leave the office. In order for the report to be meaningful it must get into the hands of all parties involved. The original typed copy of the report should be sent directly to the judge for inclusion into the family file. Copies should go to both attorneys as well, and it is my practice to send a copy to the family relations investigator or mediator involved in the matter. This can often excuse the psychologist from testifying since most family relations investigators will attach the psychological report as an exhibit to their own report. The report often comes into evidence in this manner. Of course, the psychologist will have to make a court appearance if one of the attorneys wishes to cross-examine him or her.

Most attorneys either permit their clients to read the report or provide them a copy. Attorneys have told me that since their clients pay for the report, they feel entitled to a copy. In addition, most attorneys feel that their clients have a right to know what material is being presented against or in support of their position. That way, they can better assist their attorney to prepare for the court presentation.

On the other hand, the report written for the judge and attorneys can be fairly technical in language and may be easily misunderstood by an emotional parent who sees only one side of the issue. Ideally, a parent who reads the report should have the opportunity to meet with the evaluator so that the language can be explained to him or her. This helps to clear up errors in understanding and gives the evaluator an opportunity to inform the parents about certain of the child's needs of which the parent may not be aware.

Providing parents with a copy of the evaluator's report raises a philosophical problem. It is certainly unrealistic for a psychologist to expect a parent involved in a custody dispute to read a psychological report objectively. Because the parent is intimately involved, the evaluator might have to deal with an unsophisticated, raving parent who refuses to accept the conclusions of the report. There are some circumstances in which the parent absolutely should not have access to the report. If the evaluator feels that the data is so sensitive that reading the report could cause serious emotional damage, this should be noted in the cover letter. Of course, all reports should be stamped "confidential" on the front page. It is up to the attorneys to decide whether to release the information to their clients.

All of the people involved in a custody case are entitled to a clear report. It must be well-written, and grammatically correct, with data that gives a lucid impression of the family dynamics. Specific paragraph headings should be used often to organize the content for the reader. Nothing is more disturbing than to read the summary of a report and have no idea how the writer reached those conclusions. If a report is well-written, the recommendations in the summary should come as no surprise.

Parents must realize that a psychologist needs sufficient time to write a coherent report. Most evaluators will put their data aside and reflect on it for awhile rather than write the report immediately. A few days of thinking time puts initial impressions into a rational perspective. The psychologist needs to sharpen his or her detective's eye in order to fit all the clues together and work toward an answer. A report is not ordinarily written in segments but instead is usually dictated or written in one session. The report should not be written until the evaluator knows how the data relate to the larger picture. Stories and incidents need to be cross-checked so that a complete picture of the circumstances can be presented. Close inspection and careful scrutiny of all the data will usually reveal versions of the truth perceived through a framework of strong emotion, selectivity, and bias. For example, a father might have said he wanted custody because the mother had denied him visitation rights to the child. The mother will maintain that at no time did she ever deny visitation and that, furthermore, she believes in promoting and supporting a father-son relationship. On the surface it might appear that one of these people must be lying, but careful examination reveals a different perspective. In fact, when the father came to pick up his child for his court-ordered weekend, the child was quite sick and the mother did not allow him to go out, a legitimate decision consistent with doctor's orders. The father spoke with the child for a few minutes, saw that a visit was not possible, and left without speaking to the mother, certain that she *made* his child sick just to get him angry. The father, assuming that, since he did not get visitation this weekend, he will be allowed it the next, shows up at the door for his "scheduled" visit the following Saturday. Mother, sticking to the letter of the court order (first and third weekends only to Father), has taken the child to the beach for the day. The father ends up banging on the door of an empty house, then runs to his attorney to file contempt and custody proceedings against the mother for denying him his visits. The mother is surprised to hear of the father's charges since she honestly had no intention of denying him his rights. In this circumstance neither parent has demonstrated any flexibility, concern for the child's needs, or even a simple ability to communicate with each other. This type of incident, pathetic as it may seem, is actually all too common in custody and visitation cases. If the parents had learned to communicate, cooperate, and focus on the child instead of their own needs, their misunderstanding might have easily been avoided.

Such incidents and disagreements between parents must be carefully dissected in order to fully understand the psychology of the family. Parents tend to hold fast to their biases and try very hard to prove their prejudiced positions. They are stubborn in the office and equally stubborn in the courtroom. Their defensiveness and anger often force their attorneys into ridiculous confrontations in order to prove their positions. It is not unusual to see two attorneys arguing at great length in court over which parent will get an extra hour a month with the child, or a broken television set and a twenty dollar potty chair. The parents, driven by guilt and rage, struggle to win these battles so that their individual positions can be vindicated. I have been involved in a number of custody battles where both parents were attorneys themselves. One would assume that since they are so familiar with the system, they would attempt to mediate the case and not become involved in such foolish courtroom maneuvers. In fact, my experience has indicated that attorneys are even more intransigent than laypeople, since they need to prove who is the better lawyer. This creates a miserable situation for their own attorneys and their cases often turn tragically into farces.

Since the evaluator has adopted the position of the child's advocate, it is incumbent on him or her to allot a great deal of space in the report to delineating the psychology of the child. In conjunction with this, the characteristics of the parents must be thoroughly explicated to demonstrate which one is best able to meet the needs of the child. If the report is complete, the ultimate recommendation should be almost self-evident. The central conclusion should become more and more clear as one reads through the report. Once finished, the reader should feel comfortable that the conclusion is correct.

As indicated, a psychological report on custody should have specific and direct recommendations. These should be so carefully stated that there can be no mistake as to the thrust of the report. Parents and attorneys should feel free to call on the psychologist directly for clarification if necessary. A psychologist will normally get calls from unhappy attorneys who wish to offer other information to see if it will change the conclusions, but this type of pressure will not have much effect if the data are well developed and the report is well written.

Leonard Diamond, Ph.D.
A Psychological Services Corporation

(805) 482-5166   **License No. PT3071**

Sample Report-Tests Administered

   1. DTACC Structured Interview (Adult, Child). An in-depth, structured, interview procedure aimed at understanding the patient's ability to effectively utilize social judgment, insight, and awareness. Many questions are asked to document historical information, family systems, the ability to handle problems of living, capacity for good planning and associations, progression of thought processes, emotional state, decision-making, and relationship abilities.

   2. Peabody Picture Vocabulary Test (Child). This is a nonverbal test of intelligence based on the child's sight and hearing vocabulary. The child is asked to select pictures depicting various aspects of the environment or abstract concepts. This is a power rather than a speed test. It is well standardized and offers an excellent estimate of I.Q., mental age, and percentile ranking within the child's specific age group.

   3. The Bender Visual-Motor Gestalt Test (Child). This test demonstrates whether an individual can integrate visual stimuli into a meaningful whole and reproduce them through motor action into drawings. The patient's ability to effectively integrate a given stimulus constellation composed of simple geometric figures demonstrates central nervous system integrity.

455 Rosewood Avenue Suite M
Camarillo, California 93010

4. Projective Drawings (Child). This test requires that the child draw separate pictures of a house, a tree, a person, and a family involved in some activity. The productions are then compared subjectively to normative data on many and varied groups of children with previously well-documented degrees of pathology.

5. The Rorschach Technique (Adult, Child). This test (commonly referred to as the "ink blot test") offers the client an ambiguous and unstructured set of stimuli. The client must integrate these stimuli, offer structure from within, and respond in a specified manner. The test is scored both objectively and subjectively. It can often consume a great deal of time in administration, scoring, and interpretation.

6. The Minnesota Multiphasic Personality Inventory (Adult). This is a 567-question, true-false, paper-and-pencil test. It is a forced-choice test that measures truthfulness, defensiveness, hypochondriasis, depression, hysteria, psychopathy, paranoid thinking, sexual identification, tension and anxiety, schizophrenic thinking, emotional energy level, introversion-extroversion level, repression level, ego strength, and addictive behavior. It is a valid test, scored statistically, and interpreted both in an actuarial fashion and in a clinical-subjective manner.

7. Sentence-Completion Test (Adult). This test offers the client fifty-eight incomplete sentence stems. The subject is asked to finish the sentence and the test is interpreted subjectively. The areas studied include: relationships with parents, relationships with children, anxiety level, frustration feelings, guilt, ability to make future plans, fantasy, sexual identification, and general decision-making in life experiences.

8. Symptom Checklist (Adult). This is a listing of sixty-four psychological and physical symptom constellations. The subject is asked how much these symptoms bother him or her at the present time and to respond on a scale of "not at all, a little, a lot, extremely" for each question. The data is evaluated subjectively in order to understand the subject's intra- and interpersonal discomforts.

Psychological Evaluations of the Jones Family

Psychological Evaluation: Blanche Jones (Mother)

Blanche Jones is an attractive forty-six-year-old woman who seemed moderately anxious throughout the session. This did not interfere with her ability to cooperate, and she was quite verbal and organized. She presented her side of the situation in a straightforward and coherent manner. She stated that the current issue is one of custody involving her six-year-old son, James. She and her husband separated four months ago after seven years of marriage. Her marriage to Neville Jones is her second one, and his third. She stated that she has five children from her first marriage, all in their twenties, who have left home. She feels that they have grown to be excellent adults in her custody and "for this reason I feel that I should maintain sole custody of James."

Blanche stated that when she and Neville separated, she assumed that custody would go to her or that they would establish a joint situation. At this time she finds that he is filing for sole custody of James and she is "very shocked and terribly upset." She said that James was not a planned child but that they were pleased to have him. She also feels that having James has become very much of an obsession with Neville, whom she describes as "a very dominant and aggressive person who always wanted to play the major role in child rearing." Blanche reiterated that she has brought up her other chlidren and she feels very competent as a mother. She does not see herself as inadequate in any way despite Neville's claims that she is an unfit mother. She describes him as having taken over quite insidiously by criticizing her constantly in front of the children, denigrating her abilities, and adding much fuel to the breakup of the marriage. She also feels that he imposed an enormous amount of discipline on both herself and her children at all times.

Blanche stated that her first marriage lasted for thirteen years. It gradually disintegrated because her ex-husband was extremely passive. He was not able to work or support the family and he was completely unable to take hold of normal parenting responsibilities. He was forced into bankruptcy because of his poor work skills and poor business abilities. Blanche feels strongly that this event was the ultimate blow and the undoing of the relationship.

After her first marriage, Blanche vowed to find a man who was more assertive, aggressive, and direct. These needs eventually led to her marriage to Neville Jones, as she saw in him all of the traits lacking in her previous husband. She stated that she soon found Neville to be overly demanding, strict, and extremely aggressive both verbally and physically. She feels that he placed many unreasonable demands on her and that "he had to have everything his way or nothing." She discovered approximately two years ago that she could no longer tolerate his strict demeanor and is certain that this is what led to the disintegration of the family structure. Blanche offered many examples of Neville's excessive rigidity. He would not permit her teenage children to go out in the evenings, setting their bedtime at 7:00 P.M. In addition, he would not allow any of her children to watch television but was extremely lenient with James and clearly favored James at all times.

At the height of their difficulties, Blanche and Neville went to a marriage and family counselor. She reports that her husband went to approximately two or three sessions and would not change anything or return for further counseling. He just kept repeating that she was not a good enough mother for James. She feels that Neville truly believes that she is not a stable person. She is equally certain that he is very much in error. She also said that she knows that James has many close feelings for her as well as toward his father, and she does not wish to interfere with their relationship. James has told her that his father says that she is "no good," and that he also uses a great many "four letter words" to describe her to the child. She is upset that James has directly expressed his wish to live with his father, because she feels that this would not be an appropriate placement. For the present, Blanche and Neville have shared James for one-half week each as per the existing court order. This is expected to continue for two more months, until the next hearing. Blanche says that this arrangement has not been successful. She said that her husband has James for more of the time due to difficulties in their work schedules and the change-over times. Neville is very late in returning James each time they exchange custody.

Blanche stated that James had open-heart surgery when he was approximately three years of age. He did well and now experiences no medical problems or residuals from the surgery. He is currently permitted a full range of activity and she sees him as a "normal boy."

When James was five years old, Blanche very much wanted to place him in kindergarten in a public school. Neville fought this and insisted that James be enrolled in a private school. She went ahead and placed him in public school in March of this year and reports that he has done well and will soon be placed in a year-round school. This is a 45-15 plan, where the children attend school for nine weeks and then have a three-week vacation. Blanche is certain that this twelve-month program will be very good for James but Neville disagrees. He has told her that this is not a good educational concept and that James is smarter than his teacher. "He criticizes everything, and he feels that only strict discipline is good but he is terribly inconsistent." Blanche sees herself as far more realistic and consistent with regard to her son. She is very upset at her husband, who agrees with nothing she wishes for her son and who tells her frequently that she is "incompetent and crazy."

Blanche is attempting to examine her relationship with her son and states that things have become very difficult lately. She knows that he is extremely close to his father, but she repeated many times that she loves James a great deal and has not neglected him in any way. She describes herself as an excellent mother and feels that she is involved in a "power struggle" with Neville. She is certain that he does not want her in James's life at all, and she offers as proof of this the fact that he told her many times that her own children should have no contact with their natural father. "He is of the opinion that a change-over from one parent to another is not a good process for any child." Throughout the session she repeated her anxiety over the fact that she could never please her husband because of his excessive rigidity in both ideation and actions. Now she feels that she must fight him. She has no other choice but to pursue full custody of James, because Neville "will not demonstrate any flexibility or creativity" in setting up a joint custody arrangement. She can envision sharing custody, but Neville has flatly rejected this idea. She states that not only does he not cooperate but he also ridicules her for her ideas. As an example of her attempt to share custody, she indicated that she presented a number of plans but Neville would not accept any of them. He insisted that he must have James every Saturday and Sunday and all holidays. She knows that Neville would refuse to permit her to see James even if he had to work and she had the day off. She described her husband continuously as dogmatic, rigid, and uncooperative. She also sees him as extremely obstructionistic, and says Neville "sets James up so that he is very tired and cranky when it is my turn to have him."

Blanche currently works at the Reagan County Hospital as a nurse. She has been teaching nursing at the Carter College and her semester just ended. She is a staff charge nurse at the hospital and at this time she works only on Friday and Saturday evenings from 11:00 P.M. to 7:00 A.M. She said that she intends to keep this schedule until July. In addition to her work and teaching, she is continuing to take classes toward her second Master's degree at the Ford Learning Center. When she begins to work on a full-time schedule it will be during normal day-time hours, 9:00 A.M. to 5:00 P.M. She eventually wishes to return to public health nursing or administration. She is certain that she will be able to get one of these jobs because of her wide experience, educational training, and excellent qualifications.

Blanche spoke at length with regard to the activities she shares with her son. She enjoys playing with him, going to the park and visiting museums and other educational institutions. James appears to enjoy these learning trips and Blanche shares his enjoyment. She feels that they have an excellent rapport and their home is running smoothly. She described good routines, consistent bedtimes, healthy interactions, and a good nutritional program. She is obviously sincere about her feelings for her son, as while discussing this area she was tearful and highly upset about the prospect of losing custody.

With regard to the future, Blanche stated that she wants James to be in a good school program and continue to have a wholesome family life with her as well as with his father. She feels that Neville will have to make many changes. She said many times that she is willing to work out the problems in communicating with her husband. She wants him to stop ridiculing her in front of the child and to stop trying to intimidate her. She fears that he will continue these ploys until he gets full custody of James, and this is most disturbing to her. She suspects that James does not want to live with her because of his father's influence, but she feels that it would be best for him to remain in her home. She does not want Neville's rigidity and lack of consistency to hurt James.

Throughout the session, Blanche was extremely cooperative and also very upset about the current situation. She feels blocked by Neville and admits that she has had difficulties in making decisions lately because she fears her husband's obstructionism and anger. She was highly animated and moderately anxious. Her speech was pressured at times, but there were no indications of any bizarre or inappropriate affect or ideation. She is socially skilled, insightful, and obviously bright. There were no direct manipulations noted and she was highly responsive to all of the questions asked. Insight and judgment appear intact. She was oriented in all spheres of person, place, and time. She had excellent recall for small details but did not show any excessive compulsiveness or ruminative ideation. She is creative and has a good awareness of her current legal situation. She is obviously angry at her husband and confused by his actions. She sees herself as a competent mother and nurse and apparently enjoys both roles. She appeared to believe in herself, and there is no doubt that she told the truth as she sees it. She has good future plans and is well versed in financial matters as well as independent survival skills. She is capable, able to handle the usual problems of living, and very willing to make a good home for her son.

Blanche offers an interesting Rorschach protocol. She is able to present most of the usual popular responses along with some unique and highly original responses. There are no content areas that may be considered bizarre, and the Rorschach is seen as quite healthy. She has many responses suggesting good intellect and creativity. She presents good form level and an appropriate use of other determinants, and she appears as a reality-based individual who is highly practical and ccmpetent. Blanche demonstrates some anxiety and emotionality but these are seen as in check and due to situational stressors. In summary, the Rorschach offers no evidence of disturbance.

Blanche presents a valid M.M.P.I. profile. She does not attempt to lie, fake bad, or fake good. She does not endorse any of the rare, unusual, or disturbed items and she is not at all defensive. The profile is a very accurate representation of her current personality status and none of the scales fall within the pathological range. Blanche does not internalize anxiety into hysteria, hypochondriasis, or psychosomatic difficulties. She is a woman who has the capacity to think in a highly flexible and orderly manner, and she does not place undue stress or pressure on herself from within. At this time, she shows some mild depression, but this is seen as quite situational and not at all chronic or disabling. She is bright, capable, competent, and well able to structure her environment appropriately. In addition, she shows excellent sensitivity toward her own needs and feelings as well as the needs and motives of the people around her.

On the M.M.P.I. Blanche demonstrates that she is well-identified as a female in a highly traditional sense. Although she is independent and active in her profession, she tends to endorse items suggesting that she is most comfortable as a wife, mother, and homemaker. She has a low anxiety level, and there are no suggestions of any psychotic thought processes, delusions, hallucinatory material or primary process thinking. She is not overly threatened by her environment, and she sees herself as being able to handle most life situations. She has an excellent emotional energy level. One would expect her energy level to be lower because of her situational depression and discomfort, but she is overriding the depression with her intellect. She is very bright and well able to approach her environment in a creative, efficient, and intellectual fashion. She enjoys tackling projects outside of herself, and she has the ability to follow things through to completion. At this time, Blanche endorses items suggesting that she is far more extroverted than introverted. She is dealing very effectively with both groups and individuals. She enjoys close interpersonal relationships, and she is a good discloser of personal information.

Blanche's performance on the Sentence Completion and Symptom Check List Tests does not reveal anything remarkable. She appears as a very straightforward and dynamic person who enjoys good relationships with others. She is fairly conservative in her views, and she feels particularly close to her son and her other children. She feels that she has been betrayed by Neville, who she thought would help make a stable and secure life for her. There is also distrust of other men noted, as well as strong feelings of being manipulated by authority figures. She is attempting to rise above these feelings and assert her own independence and competence. She is easily able to accept responsibility and feels good about her own abilities. She has the drive and strength to be successful on her own.

In summary, the test data do not reveal any major pathology. Blanche Jones is apparently a healthy person with excellent abilities. There is nothing documented in the testing or the history that would contra-indicate her effectiveness as a parent and role model. There is no doubt that she is a loving and caring mother.

Psychological Evaluation: Neville Jones (Father)

Neville Jones is a sixty-two-year-old man who appears considerably younger than his age. He was extremely verbal, very straightforward in his responses, very definite, and quite cooperative.
There were no indications of any resistance, and he discussed
his position in a soft-spoken manner. He is a particularly striking
man. He is quite well developed physically, handsome, and looks
to be no more than forty-five years old. He stated immediately
that the issue is one of custody and that it is critical at this time
because he feels that "James is very closely bonded to me and
not closely to Blanche." He further asserts that he and James
share many similar characteristics and that he understands his
son "better than anyone in the world." He feels that James is
unusually skillful with his hands for such a young child and that
Blanche has no mechanical skills at all. He said that his son is
brighter than Blanche. He added, "in experience and native intelligence, I outrank Blanche."

He said that when he has disagreements with his son, they
are over very quickly and end with a loving response, such as
a hug and a kiss. Neville feels that when his wife has a disagreement with James "she completely rejects him, and that is
not good for him." He feels certain that his wife is a very angry
person and has constantly rejected both himself and his son. He
also feels bad that he does not have enough time to share more
activities with James. Now that James is learning to swim, Neville
wants to take him to the pool in his apartment complex on a
daily basis. He also wants to expose his son to sailing and tumbling.
He was a part-time tumbling instructor for twelve years, and
he "can help James to be better coordinated." He made no attempts
to cover up any of his desires, and he said directly that he wants
"full control of him." He does not want James being involved
in any team sports right now as his wife does, because, "statistics
show that too many joint injuries occur at this age."

Neville stated that he married Blanche after they had known
each other approximately two years. He feels that the relationship

was quite good in the initial stages but it rapidly broke down. He said that the turning point came when Blanche took her first husband back to court for an increase in support for the children of her marriage to him still living at home. At that time, the first husband "started brainwashing her kids, they got on her, and she got on me." Neville explained that he could not tolerate "the interference of this man in my family." He was obviously quite jealous of Blanche's first husband, and he was angry at his wife. He felt that she had no right forcing this stranger to surface again due to a court action which she initiated.

He feels that his wife is not a good mother, since she had sent one of her sons to live with a relative so that he would avoid going to Juvenile Hall. Another son was suspended from school for throwing a board eraser at a teacher. He felt that he had to be very strict with her children, and he set up rigid schedules for them. "Due to these schedules, things began to shape up nicely." Neville set up behavioral contracts with his stepchildren, and got them involved in gardening and home-improvement projects. He feels that the family was progressing well under his strong leadership. He was upset when his wife's first husband began to "sabotage" his relationship with the children; he is certain that this actually took place. It was at this time that Blanche began to "side with the kids against me," and communications broke down. They did attempt family and marriage counseling but he felt impatient and angry and decided to leave the home. During the time of this separation, he has had James with him for approximately one-half the time and frequently more than half due to the frequent changes in Blanche's work schedule. He feels that the longer he can spend with James, the easier it will be to undo his wife's bad influence.

Neville feels that splitting the custody of his son has not worked well even though they live only two blocks from each other. He states that his wife keeps changing the dates on him and trying to get James for more time. They have a problem now because she wishes to take James on a one-week vacation. Neville is uncomfortable with this because, "she and her kids are not great drivers and I don't want James killed or injured." When asked if he felt that he was somewhat overprotective, he stated that he is "definitely not" being overprotective but that he has "twenty-two years with drivers and teaching defensive driving." Because of this, he is sure that he is very knowledgeable in the area and that he can recognize poor driving when he sees it.

With regard to James, Neville feels that they have "an extremely excellent bonding and relationship." He states that he knows of only one other relationship that is as close or as good. This is his relationship with his older daughter. He has a thirty-three-year-old son, a thirty-two-year-old son, and a thirty-year-old daughter in addition to his "special" thirty-five-year-old daughter. He enjoys closeness with all of his children and outlined many activities which he does with them as well as with James. He feels that he and James share a myriad of interests, and he enjoys exposing James to new learning activities, sports, and play. He enjoys being with him and has the luxury of spending much time with James since he is now retired.

Neville stated many times that his wife is a poor manager in all ways. He recalled that she was an instructor in family planning and birth control and that they had agreed that they would not have any more children. He offers as an example of her poor managing skill the fact that she became pregnant. Neville stated that James tells him that he loves him a great deal and that he does not love his mother. As an example of this, he indicated with great glee the fact that James would frequently "get into her things and mess them up in order to get back at her." He feels that James is angry because of Blanche's treatment of him, and he stated that very early in James's life she would "throw him in the playpen or the crib and often hit him with a ruler." He does admit that James has some positive feelings for his mother and knows that his constant negative input about her confuses James at times. He is angry at Blanche for using techniques such as locking James in the bathroom for time-out periods as punishment for acting-out. Neville feels that James should not be exposed to his wife or her children because they are chronically in trouble and "she doesn't use her head very much."

Neville said that he is far more responsive, expressive, sensitive, and able to interact more effectively as a parent than Blanche. He also feels that he is far more interested in their son and he denies ever lying or being too rigid. He feels that he listens and is flexible. Blanche's claims and examples of his rigidity were discussed thoroughly and he denies being overly obstructionistic. He has reasons for his behavior in all of the events she cited. When questioned about his excessive use of profanity, he admits that he used it regularly but only in response to the frustration his wife created for him. He regrets using so many expletives in front of James. He added that his wife is equally guilty of using profanity against him but not in front of the child.

Neville was married twice prior to this marriage. The first relationship lasted twenty-six years. He stated that his first wife had "emotional problems" and this was responsible for the marriage ending. The second marriage was very brief and was terminated by Neville because "of her need to be with other men," which he could not tolerate.

Neville has just retired from his job as overseas export manager for Nixon Industries. He had many responsibilities, his major job being to ensure that all departments ran smoothly and to troubleshoot problems regarding inventory, orders, and personnel. He has also been involved in teaching such topics in his spare time as defensive driving, tumbling, winemaking, and music. He now has plans to return to school on a part-time basis and looks forward to becoming certified as a pediatric physical therapist. He wishes to have the opportunity to work in this field as he very much enjoys being with children. Neville stated that he has a great deal of property as well as other business interests. This will ensure that he will continue to be financially well off while retired and pursuing a new career. He also wishes to spend more time sailing, traveling, and taking extended trips with his son on holidays. He wants sole custody of James and is willing to offer "liberal visitation on an alternate weekend basis" to Blanche.

Throughout the session, Neville was very cooperative, calm, and straightforward. There were many indications of overt animosity toward his wife. It is clear that he neither likes nor trusts her. He made such statements without expressing much anger but it is apparent that he is quite bitter with regard to this custody struggle. He feels that at one point in their separation, his wife was willing to give James to him and he cannot understand why others do not immediately see that he is a far more appropriate parent than she. Neville demonstrated a wide range of emotion and there were no direct suggestions of bizarre ideation. He is a nonanxious individual who was clear in thought and speech.

Neville brought with him a letter from a psychiatrist he had consulted with James. It does state that he and James have "an unusually close bonding." He brought this concept up many times during the session. He also brought pictures of James enjoying activities with him and he stated that this was a good illustration of their relationship. He was not overly manipulative but he was very definite in all of his statements and tried to leave no room for doubt. He is obviously a very bright individual but he is also obviously quite rigid in his ideas and in statements concerning his son. He was oriented in all spheres and moderately compulsive. He is apparently a creative person with wide-ranging interests and many skills. He has been involved in many side businesses during his career and has demonstrated expertise and excellent success in every area he has attempted. He is quite chauvinistic in his approach to women and made many sexist comments about Blanche and about women in general. He tells the truth as he sees it. He is very involved with his own needs and plans as well as plans for his son's future. He is capable of demonstrating affection. His self-image is exceptionally good, if not somewhat inflated and narcissistic. He does not accept the limitations of others well. He expects everyone to be highly responsible at all times, but he is most definitely capable of close and depth-oriented interpersonal relations. His future plans appear as unique, appropriate, and creative. They are somewhat symbolic in that he does feel that he can "mold" the present and future of children. Whether he pursues this or not, his financial future is assured through his many investments and skills.

Neville Jones presents a very creative and unique Rorschach protocol. He utilizes all of the areas on the blots and gives a high number of responses, most of them well detailed and complex. He is moderately compulsive and highly intellectual. The test does not offer any evidence of frank or debilitating pathology. He is able to see the world in both macro- and microscopic fashion. He is extremely aware of nuances in interpersonal relationships and is quite controlling in his approach to others. He does show depth of feeling and a good potential for more flexibility in the range of his responses to others. He also shows anger at females throughout his responses. He feels that he is far more accomplished and qualified in more areas than most women. However, there are enough responses to indicate that it is possible for him to have his consciousness raised and learn new values. He demonstrates disappointment in women and this appears to be the root of his defensive chauvinism.

Neville produces a valid M.M.P.I. profile where he does not attempt to lie, fake bad, or fake good. He is not overly defensive; his profile is unique and generally seen as highly competent. His neurotic scales are low and he does not internalize anxiety into psychosomatic or hypochondriacal difficulties. He denies feelings of depression and sees such feelings as highly noxious. He does place some stress on himself from within, but the test shows that he can be flexible in his thinking. His rigidity comes through when he takes stands on issues and cannot be moved, but the M.M.P.I. suggests that he is capable of entertaining many different ideas and alternatives. He is very bright and is an excellent manipulator of his environment. He is able to structure the world around him so that he can be successful. He is able to do so by virtue of a high degree of sensitivity and awareness of the needs of other people. He is moderately suspicious, but this is not seen as pathological and he does not appear as paranoid in any way.

Neville is well identified as a male. Although so many of his verbalizations are chauvinistic, the M.M.P.I. scale reveals that he is not basically traditional in all of his perceptions. He is able to produce many feelings of closeness, warmth, and tenderness along with other feelings that may be considered feminine. He is very well read, highly aesthetic, extremely eager in all of his activities, and sensitive and very skilled at relating. He denies feeling anxiety from the external world because he sees the environment as not offering any stress that cannot be dealt with successfully. He does not feel any threat and there are no suggestions of schizophrenic ideation or disturbance in thinking. His emotional energy level is very high. Not only is he extremely intellectual and efficient, but he is also moderately rebellious. He enjoys dealing with the environment in a very direct fashion, and he can be quite tactless at times; but he always gets the job done. He demonstrates a high amount of ability to stick to a task until completion. He does not like to delegate authority and instead takes charge and presses ahead to his goal. He is tenacious, mildly antagonistic, and very direct. He endorses items suggesting that he has excellent social interactions with both groups and individuals. He is extroverted, able to charm others, and able to relate on a close level. The M.M.P.I. profile is healthy and dynamic; he is obviously a man who has a great deal of love and care for his child. There is no doubt that he is honest in his relationship with his son and equally honest in his feeling that he is a good parent. The M.M.P.I. shows no pathology to dispute his parenting abilities.

On the Sentence Completion Test, Neville clearly demonstrates his need to convince others of the poor performance exhibited by his wife as a parent and of his own ability to be an excellent parent. Almost all of his statements refer to the current situation and his attempt to gain sole custody of James. There are no signs of disturbance in these statements, but he is of one mind at this time. He is gathering all of his energies to make this campaign to discredit his wife successful. He does not endorse any debilitating symptoms on the Symptom Check

List. He is willing to admit to some situational discomfort and anxiety associated with the legal dispute. Nothing in the data demonstrates lack of competence in parenting. Although he is rigid in his approach, he does have the potential to examine many different ideas, and he shows excellent warmth and caring skills.

Psychological Evaluation: James O. Jones (5 years, 11 months)

Behavioral Observations

James is a small, very cute little boy who was highly verbal and appropriate throughout the session. He was cooperative, but he also demonstrated an occasional obstructionistic tendency when he did not know an answer or when he became tired of a test. His attention span was good, but he required regular reinforcement in the form of positive statements about his performance. When he became agitated, he was offered more structure and was then able to follow through with the tasks presented. He was fully aware of when he was giving correct answers, and he did not like not knowing answers. James has a full awareness of the situation between his parents. He was eager to speak to the custody issue, and he had been well prepared for the testing by both his mother and his father. He understood the role of the examiner and established a warm rapport very quickly. He stated many times that he wants to talk to the judge and that he was happy that his statements would be carried to the judge in the report of the testing.

James currently attends public school and is in a kindergarten-first-grade combined class. He said quite vigorously that he does not like his school, his classroom, or his teacher. When questioned quite thoroughly about this position regarding school, he was not able to offer any reasons. When asked if he says this because he knows that his father is not in favor of public schools, he freely admitted that this was the reason. He knows his teacher's name, mother's address, father's address, and both of their phone numbers. He counts to one hundred with no difficulty, can recite the alphabet with no errors, and knows all of the colors. There is no doubt that James is learning in school despite his statement that he does not like anything. He also discussed the fact that he has acted-out on occasion in school and created problems for himself and his teacher. This has been handled with the use of time-out periods in a cubicle in the corner of the room. James feels that he has many close friends in his class and that he has no trouble learning new material.

James looks forward to going to school in the morning each day and to seeing his friends. Despite his statement that he disliked his teacher, he sees her as helpful, caring, and supportive most of the time. He has bad feelings about creating problems by talking out of turn or fighting. James stated that when he is with his mother, she walks him to the corner and he then walks two blocks to school. When he is with his father, he is driven to school. He likes to walk because he meets his friends and he does not understand why his father has to drive him every morning. He has not discussed this with his father. When I told him that it would be all right to tell his father that he prefers to walk, he smiled and stated that he would take care of this immediately. When he comes home from school he has set routines at both homes, which include chores, playtime and time spent with his parents. He feels that this goes well and has complaints only about bedtime at his mother's home, which he feels is too early.

Although James has many friends, he rarely spends much time at anyone's home. He feels that such behavior is not supported by either parent and he knows that both parents are highly protective of him. James briefly discussed his stepbrothers and stepsisters. Since they do not live at home at this time, he does not feel very attached to them. He does enjoy seeing them for visits, and he knows where each one lives and what each does. He knows that the older boys who live close by are usually "on call" for babysitting or to help his mother when she needs them. He feels that they are not overly interested in him. He discussed the relationships in a manner that suggests that he is tolerated but is not anyone's special favorite. He states that his mother's children get along well with her but do not talk to his father. His father's children get along well with both parents. James is clear that the battle lines have been drawn between his parents and their children as well.

James stated that his parents rarely entertained other adults in the home. They did sometimes go out to dinner but not with close friends. He stated that his mother has friends from work but his father does not. When questioned about his favorite friend in the world, James stated that it was his dog. He has a poodle that he takes care of, occasionally takes with him from home to home, and enjoys talking to when they are alone together.

When questioned about his relationship with his father, James became quite animated. He stated that he does many things with Neville such as going to amusement parks. James then spontaneously added that he knows his parents have gotten a divorce, and above all, he wants to live with his father. He has a snake at his father's home, and he said, "I like my snake and I like my daddy the best because he lets me do anything." He said his mother lets him "do nothing except stay at home and eat peas." His father does not force this on him but, instead, "Daddy feeds me anything I want, like pudding, TV dinners, and stuff like that." He said that his father never yells at him but his mother does, and that this means "she is mean to me." James spoke in very positive terms about his father. He sees his father as quite a perfect person who does everything right and needs no changing. However, when specifics were discussed, such as being driven to school, he admitted that his father could make some improvements. His home routine with his father is not quite as lax as he makes it sound. He does have chores, bedtime, playtime, and learning time. His father helps him with schoolwork, and James says that they spend too much time with this activity.

Neville obviously places a very high emphasis on achievement, and he expects James always to be the best in everything. James enjoys this but also feels the pressure. He explained that his father does not go to his school, because he does not like public schools.

His father has made this very clear to James and has also promised him that he will go to a private school next year. James feels strongly that his father loves him, and they spend much time in physical play together. He also describes many tender and loving moments with his father.

When questioned about his relationship with his mother, James expressed many positive feelings for her as well. He stated that she takes him to the park and they spend much time together playing. She also brings other children over to play with him, and he enjoys this. His mother helps in James's classroom in school, and he feels very proud of the fact that she gives her time in this way. He also sees her as somewhat restrictive, in that she insists that he eat his meals, which consist of both meat and vegetables. Although James was very clear during the entire session that he wants to live with his father, he also expressed much love for his mother. His statements were often highly contradictory. He would explain how "mean" his mother is but in the next sentence would tell how great he feels she is. James obviously loves his mother, and is highly conflicted about having made a rigid choice to live with his father. He is also well aware of the love his mother has for him.

James stated that his parents do not get along with each other. He volunteered that, "Daddy says bad words about Momma, but I won't tell the words because he said that nobody else should know." When questioned as to why he felt that these feelings exist between his parents, James became angry and said that he did not know and he did not care. He is quite obviously aware that he is the central focus of the fight, and he fears the power he has in this situation. When questioned as to what he thinks the outcome of the difficulties will be, he shouted, "The judge is a bunch of baloney and shouldn't decide. I'm going to live with Dad and not Momma." James became highly agitated at this point, and he refused to answer anything further with regard to his relationship with parents or their relationship to each other.

When asked what three wishes he would like to have, James stated:

1. "I know what I want but it's bad and you won't like it." He was assured that anything he had to say was acceptable, and he offered the fact that he wants "a naked lady." When asked why he made this particular choice, he was quite pensive, and he said a number of times that he does not know what he would do with a naked lady but he would surely like to have one of his own. Further questioning revealed that he had seen *Playboy* magazine in his father's home as well as in his mother's home (brought in by her sons). He likes the centerfold pictures, is sexually stimulated by them, and feels that "this would be nice to have."

2. "All the candy I could eat."

3. "All the money and toys in the world."

James's second and third wishes are quite standard for his age. His first wish is quite unusual. It appears that he is trying very hard to identify with the males in his environment.

James is right-handed, right-footed and left-eyed, which is within the normal range for his age group, and he does not demonstrate any serious signs of mixed dominance. His eyes track correctly and accommodate to the same point. There were no obvious signs of organicity. His gait is excellent, and his gross muscle coordination appears to be very much intact. He was cooperative throughout the session and only became agitated when asked for more information about his relationship with his parents. James attempted all of the psychological tests presented to him and he showed no major resistance, hostility, or defiance. He appeared to enjoy himself very much, and at the end of the session he was tired but asked when he could return to "play more games." His social skills were excellent, and he related more as an adult than as a child. He exhibited excellent thought processes, associations, and judgment during the testing. He was oriented in all three spheres of person, place, and time, and had unusually good information recall. It was apparent from James's relationship skills that he is very bright. His creativity, imagination, and maturity are quite striking. James demonstrated much emotion, told the truth, and appeared to have good affective depth.

Data Analysis

James is an unusually intelligent young boy who exceeded the ceiling level on the Peabody Picture Vocabulary Test. This test is not sensitive enough for him because he is so bright; it places his I.Q. well into the Very Superior range. He is in the ninety-ninth percentile for his age group and the test yields a mental age of well over eleven years old. It is obvious that James is highly aware of his world and his mental age exceeds his chronological age by more than five years. He has exceptional sensitivity to small details and nuances in his environment. In addition, his abstraction skills are highly mature.

James's Bender performance is not commensurate with his intellectual abilities. If he had concentrated more intensely he would not have made such a high number of errors. He has difficulty with closure and angulation of figures. This may suggest some visual-motor and coordination problems. His neurological growth and development lag somewhat behind his chronological age but it is expected that this will level off as he matures. It would be helpful to involve James in some fine muscle activities and training. This could take the form of bead stringing, clay play, card games, or identifying different objects with various tactile values. The cognitive data do not demonstrate the presence of any severe or disabling organicity or brain pathology. A mild visual-motor coordination problem is noted and should be followed up in school.

James's projective drawings are good from an aesthetic viewpoint, but they do reveal mild to moderate emotional difficulties. His house drawing is ungrounded, barren, and of poor perspective. He was unclear about whether he wanted to draw his mother's home or his father's home, even though he was told to "draw a picture of a house." (He could have solved his problem by not drawing either parent's home.) He showed much physical tension while making this drawing, which turned out to be an attempt at a composite between both homes. His anxiety associated with familial relationships is quite clear because he is torn between two very angry and competitive parents. He hears them ridiculing each other, which is obviously not appropriate behavior as evidenced by James's high anxiety. James's tree drawing is also poorly grounded, very frenzied, and of poor perspective. He has an enormous knothole in the trunk, and the tree exudes feelings of stress.

When asked to draw a picture of a person, he produced a stick figure. He stated that it was a male named "Sneakers" (which is his snake's name). When asked how old this person might be, he said that he is "'finity years old," and he understood the concept of infinity. James's family drawing showed himself, his mother, and his father driving in a car. The parents were in the front and James is in the back alone, quite far from the parents as the car appears to be a long limousine. He expressed distance, anxiety, and uncertainty with regard to his parents. It is often noted in young children that when they see their parents so bitterly engaged in battle, they fear them both.

James's Rorschach protocol was poor. He felt very uncomfortable and immobilized, which prevented him from offering much internal structure to the blots. He did not like the test and although he tried, he did not produce many responses. One would expect a high number of responses from a boy who has such high intellectual skills. He was able to elaborate some percepts, but they were all fraught with hostility. He was also negative, debilitated in his percepts, anxiety-ridden, and quite explosive in his emotionality. There is no doubt that James suffers from the friction between his parents. At this time his difficulty can be described as a moderately severe generalized anxiety reaction, situationally based. Although this is interfering with his adjustment, it is my opinion that he does not require any immediate psychotherapeutic intervention. An early decision with regard to custody, along with cooperation between his parents, would help to dissipate his tensions and fearfulness. When James was offered toy families, he constructed many scenes in which the child was on the periphery while the parents argued and tugged at the child from both sides. James feels that he is literally the object of an adult tug-o-war.

Summary and Recommendations:

In summary, we have a very difficult situation that has produced high degrees of friction, misunderstanding, and total lack of trust between Blanche and Neville Jones. Blanche sees Neville as an extremely rigid and obstructionistic person, but he produced data indicating that he has a potential for warm, cooperative, and flexible feelings. He sees his wife as ineffective, unresponsive to the child's needs, and generally incompetent as a parent in all ways. This is not borne out by her data. In fact, her test data suggest that she is a very competent person who does not demonstrate any difficulties that would interfere with effective parenting skills. She loves her son and does very well with him. Despite being somewhat overprotective of James, she is allowing him to thrive and grow. Neville's data also demonstrates the same quality of material. He, too, is highly competent, bright, and overprotective, but an excellent guardian for this child. James is identified with his father because Neville is quite verbal and dominant and he has attempted to program some of James's responses. James is also well identified with his mother, and has a healthy relationship with her with the exception of repeating the negative statements of his father. Both people appear to be quite wrong with regard to their assessment of each other.

These parents live in close geographical proximity to each other. James would not be able to understand a situation in which one of his parents had sole custody while the other only had visitation rights. At this time he frequently walks from one house to the other. James is a very bright boy who is experiencing enormously high anxiety levels due to his parents' manipulations and demands, and their constant games of one-upmanship. He is being seriously victimized by the circumstances and I am certain that neither parent wishes this tension for their son. However, they are both guilty of producing it and equally responsible for perpetuating this stress.

Although Neville and Blanche have fought long and hard, it is obvious to me through the data that a joint legal custody

THE PSYCHOLOGICAL REPORT   121

and joint physical custody arrangement can work. This would be the most effective program to meet James's needs for both parents. In order to do this, the parents must shift the focus from their own needs, accept a joint-custody relationship, and learn to make peace. They must abandon their own petty grievances and anger and work toward the health and best interests of their son. A time-sharing agreement can be worked out with cooperation. If this is carefully done and maintained, the parents can achieve all of the goals they have established. A coparenting, time-sharing agreement will enhance James's mental health. The half-week with each parent as it is now constituted does not work because it places too much stress on James and makes him a visitor in each home. Just when he feels some measure of adjustment, the bottom falls out again and he has to form a new attachment in a different home. This leads to heightened anxiety, frustration, and the possibility of his acting these feelings out.

Both Neville and Blanche have constraints on their time. Even though Neville is retired, he is entering a school program to pursue a new occupation. From both a psychological and physical environmental perspective, neither parent appears to have a distinct edge over the other. It is my opinion that if they are open to sharing, they could work out a strong contract and arrive at a truce between them in the services of creating good mental health in their child. In this way they could assure that James will benefit from the best each has to offer. It is also my opinion that both parents must examine their ideas about the other and make modifications so that they can be more realistic and less angry. Neville's bravado is destructive. He must learn to trust that his wife also has the best interests of their son in mind. The only way these people can work through their negative feelings is with a neutral, third-person arbitrator (not their individual attorneys). Since they state repeatedly that they are sincerely concerned with the welfare of their child and are both intelligent people, there is no doubt that such an arrangement can be realized.

At this time the data do not support one parent over the other. These two people must realize that they have an obligation to be supportive of both each other and James. Therefore, it is my strong opinion that the court should instruct Neville and Blanche to write a coparenting contract that will assist in solving James's anxieties. This will also serve to remove the family from further hostile and damaging litigation. Their differences can be resolved by replacing stubbornness and anger with intellect and cooperation. If they so desire, I would be happy to assist in writing such a contract with them. The data clearly recommend a joint legal and joint physical custodial relationship.

Leonard Diamond, Ph.D.

This report was submitted to the judge, the attorneys, and the family-relations mediator. Both parents were shocked. They had been led by their attorneys to assume that one would emerge as a "winner" and one would have to go down to defeat. Both had mixed feelings about the positive and negative aspects of the recommendation. On the positive side, the report recommended that James have two fully functioning parents with whom he could be comfortable. On the negative side, neither parent would be able to dictate the terms. Instead, they would have to cooperate to settle their differences, and make peace with each other. These parents were both very bright and eventually reason won out. They decided to give the contracting process a try, which was strongly supported by their respective attorneys. The judge ordered them to work out a contract within two months and then return to court for a review. They did in fact meet in my office and, after approximately fourteen hours that included much therapy and consciousness-raising, were able to hammer out a contract that everyone felt they could live with and enjoy. This contract appears in one of the later sections of this book.

Parents concerned with custody should use this case as a

good example of how contact with the evaluator can be transformed from evaluation to mediation and arbitration. My experience has been that even when a recommendation may initially be reviewed as negative, many parents will be willing to return to attempt the process of contracting. This permits the evaluator to play a continuing role with the family through regular follow-up evaluations. This also serves to keep the attorneys and judge continually informed and keeps the court record updated (for the protection of the child) if the case should ever come up again.

Consultation with Attorneys After the Report

Issues of dissolution and custody are usually highly volatile and emotional, and frequently result in much acting out of hostility on the part of both parents. One man sawed all of his household furniture in half and took half of his wife's underwear and clothes after his divorce. This admittedly drastic incident demonstrates how people can react when they are forced to leave the structure of a relationship with only half of their hard-earned assets. Because of the special intensity that inheres when the custody of a child is at stake, attorneys will frequently be closely identified with their clients and become very ego-involved. Of course, any attorney reading this might immediately protest that such behavior is quite unprofessional and deny that it ever happens. However, practice differs significantly from theory, and attorneys become emotionally involved far more frequently than one might imagine.

An attorney with a high emotional investment in the father's rights movement, for example, will certainly become intensely involved with the case of his male clients. Similarly, an attorney who identifies strongly with the women's movement may identify strongly with female clients. For example, the mother such an attorney represents might be unskilled and might have sacrificed herself for many years while her husband blossomed in the professional world. He becomes a multicolored butterfly who feels that he is married to a drab and colorless caterpillar and wants out of the relationship. The woman will make a very convincing argument for her position, and her attorney will fight for that position. All of these feelings of allegiance to the client are an inevitable part of each of us, and frequently emerge in attorneys who engage in ongoing, volatile, and bitter custody fights.

When attorneys read the psychologist's report, they do so from two points of view. First, they want to offer the best possible representation of their clients. They want a favorable report from the psychologist to support the case. This way they will be able to move ahead to prove that their clients's positions are correct. Second, as involved participants, they want the approval of the court-appointed authority. In this way the theoretical position the attorneys have adopted will be vindicated and they can "deliver" for their clients, which reinforces their own ego involvement.

It is a given that both parents and both attorneys are biased individuals. The psychologist-evaluator and the judge, on the other hand, are theoretically unbiased. Therefore, when the evaluator consults with the attorneys it is important to keep in mind that each attorney sees the facts through his or her client's eyes. Oftentimes, after the attorney receives the report and reviews it with his or her client, s/he will arrange a meeting with the psychologist and try to present facts that did not come out in the evaluation, in an attempt to change the evaluator's mind. For example, the attorney might ask, "Doctor, you supported the father in this matter and I wonder if it would change your mind to know that he was once arrested for car theft." Such questions or assertions should be viewed as loaded, and the evaluator should make it a point to ask follow-up questions. Rather than offer any new opinions, the evaluator should analyze the new data, and establish the facts. A good question to ask might be, "When did this happen and what was the result?" The attorney might sheepishly admit that the incident took place twenty-six years ago and that the father was acquitted. The data can now take its place in proper perspective with the other material collected. Sometimes this type of information will shock the evaluator because he or she might not have thought to ask about any difficulties with the law. Any information gathered after the report has been submitted should be carefully weighed and considered. It is most certainly possible that one of the parties lied and that the additional information might be quite significant. If a parent or an attorney feels that the psychologist should know about something that was not previously considered, this should be communicated since it will probably be brought out in court. If it is truly important an addendum to the report can be written that takes into account the significance of this new information.

In order to keep lines of communication clear and maintain professional integrity, it is a good practice for the evaluator to consult with both attorneys whenever asked to meet with one. When an attorney calls for a consultation specifically because s/he disagrees with the conclusion of the report, a session with both attorneys can be convened to clear the air, or, if one lawyer does not agree to this, the other attorney can take a deposition from the evaluator, or can question the evaluator during the course of formal cross-examination. It is not appropriate for an evaluator to discuss a case informally with an attorney, since everything that is said is still "on the record." Such a "chat" is often well orchestrated. Psychologists should be wary of the attorney who says that he or she is "just an old country lawyer who doesn't understand all of these big words." As trite as it sounds, this kind of statement is heard with great regularity. A psychologist who hears this must be careful. S/he should defuse the situation by meeting with both attorneys and possibly both clients and then immediately running to Mother's arms for safety.

Not long ago I had the misfortune of "chatting" in the hall of the courthouse with an attorney who was upset because I did not support his client in my report. This was during a break during a case in which I was testifying at the time. The attorney said that he could not believe that his client was as passive and noncommunicative as I had reported him to be. He asked if it had anything to do with the fact that the client was an engineer and researcher for so many years. The attorney was a close friend and in a lax moment I joked that his client had an "engineer personality" and could relate to facts, numbers, and test tubes, but not to people. We both laughed, had a cup of tea, and returned to the courtroom for the remainder of my testimony. The attorney immediately proceeded to grill me relentlessly on my "extreme bias" against engineers because I had been heard to make a reference that suggested stereotyped thinking concerning the so-called "engineer personality." Frequently, an offhand remark can lead to such grief.

Parents who are supported by the evaluation still have work to do with their attorneys and should not feel that the case has been won. The judge is not bound by the recommendations of the report, especially if s/he feels that other data is more compelling. Parents should meet with their attorneys and psychologists to prepare for the introduction of the relevant testimony. A well-prepared and conscientious attorney will want to spend time with the psychologist prior to the testimony in order to indicate what facts the attorney hopes to bring out and what questions should be asked. This type of consultation is certainly appropriate and can lead to a most stimulating display of courtroom strategy. The attorney knows what the judge should hear and can help the evaluator to structure the important data to that end. This information can then be presented in a coherent and manageable form. In addition, the attorney will be prepared to rehabilitate the testimony after the cross-examination. A thorough discussion of the attorney's "game plan" is a useful move. At this time it will become plain to the attorney as to where the psychologist's testimony is weak or unsupported so that they do not get surprised in court. Some attorneys wait until five minutes before the hearing to talk with the psychologist. Obviously, this is not an advisable practice. The client, attorney, and psychologist should all meet so that all aspects of the court presentation can be discussed, rehearsed, and thoroughly analyzed.

A psychologist working in a small community quickly gets to know all the attorneys who practice family law. Friendships develop, but they cannot be permitted to interfere with the case at hand. A psychologist who does enough evaluations will eventually find him- or herself on both supporting and opposing sides of every attorney at one time or another. This is actually a healthy position to be in, since the attorneys will come to view the psychologist as an honest and unbiased professional. The clients can feel confident that they will get an objective evaluation and that friendships will not interfere with the outcome of the case. All consultations with attorneys and clients should be open, clear, technical, and specific to the case. The attorney and the psychologist share a common talent in that words and communication lie at the heart of both their professions.

5

Fees

How Fees for Custody Evaluations are Set and Collected

The fact that the practice of psychology is a business is rarely considered by either clients or psychologists. Most psychologists are relatively naive and totally unprepared to deal with fees. When one is in a helping profession, a discussion of money can seem a mundane, or even "dirty" thing to do. Graduate schools perpetuate this by purposely not preparing the budding psychologist to be an effective business person. Most beginning private practitioners do not know how to keep records, send bills, deal with insurance companies, or handle money.

Fees for a custody evaluation usually depend on how much time an evaluator puts in with the clients. This is factored through the locally accepted rates that dictate what a psychologist's time is worth. In New York City, Los Angeles, Chicago, and other large cities, fees may range upwards of $100 to $150 per hour for custody evaluations. In smaller, more rural areas, fees will tend to be lower. Psychologists must set fees with the local economy in mind so that they won't price themselves out of the market.

Parents can check with the local county psychological association for an idea of the fees charged in their specific area. Prior to visiting the psychologist, the parent should definitely establish the fee rate and the manner of payment. This should be done explicitly in order to avoid misunderstandings. A conscientious psychologist will also serve as the collector of the fee rather than leaving it to a secretary or other office personnel.

The custody evaluator must be fully paid before the report leaves the office. Once the report is sent, there is usually a dissatisfied party. If that party still owes money, it may never be collected. Therefore, the parent should fully understand at the beginning of the evaluation not only what the fees are but that they need to be collected before the report can be made public. This policy should always be enforced. Often an attorney will promise that the fees will be paid out of a later property settlement or that the "other side" will be paying the bill. This may be an honest statement on the part of the attorney but it does not pay the psychologist's bills. Payment arrangements should be made in writing so that all parties understand their responsibilities.

To summarize, fees should be set based on the amount of time spent and the local fee schedule as the main criteria. Once this has been done, the evaluators should make sure fees are collected before the report is publicly released. This should be clearly understood by all, and adhered to so that the business aspects of the matter do not become confused with the psychological aspects. Psychologists need to break with the "ivory tower" image of their field and realize that in terms of running a business, being a psychologist is no different than being a plumber or carpenter. Most grocery stores do not allow credit; neither should psychologists.

Custody Anger—Dealing with Complaints, Threats, and Lawsuits

A small number of people who engage in custody battles become very disturbed. They will return to court over and over, trying to seek some satisfaction and get the court to sanction their position. Their disturbance grows and rational processes deteriorate as the stress of the confrontations mount. When they lose in court, they cannot accept the fact that they do not have a legitimate case. Instead, they externalize their anger against the attorney who handled the case, the judge who tried the case, or the psychologist who evaluated the case. Angry letters or calls are part of the business and should just be accepted. The parent certainly has the right to be unhappy, and the attorney and evaluator must permit this person to vent his or her feelings without becoming defensive or argumentative themselves. The facts, in any case, will have little meaning at such times since the parent would be arguing from personal conviction and bias. It is sufficient for the psychologist to remind the parent in a calm manner that the concerns of everyone in this situation are with the needs of the child and everyone is doing their best.

Parents should be cautioned not to overreact. In order for a parent to plan for the future in a rational manner, the decision of the court must be accepted.

At times, angry parents will go further than just a simple letter or abusive call. Complaints or formal grievances are sometimes made to newspapers, judges, or to professional associations. These are almost always inappropriate and costly in terms of time, energy, and money. The most bizarre complaints still require follow-up by professional associations and a great deal of documentation is required from all sides. For example, once, in a fairly traditional and straightforward custody matter, the father was upheld in court and received sole custody of his daughter. The mother, on one of her scheduled visitations, kidnapped the child, moved to the mountains, and lived in a shack with her. When the husband found her and regained custody, the mother filed a complaint both against her attorney for malpractice and also against the court-appointed psychologist. She said that the psychologist manipulated the data, and forced her to take tests in a room with uncomfortable chairs where loud music was being played. She charged furthermore that the psychologist lied in court about important facts and was abusive and hostile to her in private. Of course none of these charges could be easily proven or disproven. The respective ethics committees investigated both the attorney and psychologist, a lengthy and involved process during which evidence had to be produced to prove the instability of the individual making the complaint. The attorney and psychologist were eventually cleared completely but they had to endure a long, tedious, anxiety-producing process. The mother received no real satisfaction from any of this. Since this type of nonsense does occur I again caution parents against overreacting since they could open themselves to a libel or slander suit. Needless to say, the psychologist should be careful to document information about interactions with his or her clients, and these should be filed carefully.

Threats and lawsuits can be avoided if parents will attempt to set aside their anger and communicate honestly with the professionals. It is possible for people in dispute to come to agreements if they deal with each other on a rational basis. Neither attorneys nor psychologists should attempt to deal with threats or court actions alone. Instead, they too should consult a trained attorney who knows how to protect them from external complaints as well as from themselves.

6

The Courtroom

General Courtroom Decorum

The courtroom is a very special and unique place. Lay persons and professionals both often feel very threatened by the courtroom but this does not have to be the case. If one knows the rules, which are fairly specific, and carefully follows them, one will feel less anxious. These rules are more often than not unwritten and one must be aware of how to conduct oneself appropriately. If you are a witness in a case, the following scenario is typical.

Initially, you will be called to the witness stand by the attorney. Prior to taking the stand you will appear in front of the clerk who sits adjacent to the judge's bench. The clerk will administer the oath. This oath takes slightly different forms in different counties or states, but usually goes something like: "Please raise your right hand. In the matter before the court at this time, do you solemnly swear to tell the truth, the whole truth and nothing but the truth, so help you God?" You will answer, "I do," and then will be told to take your seat on the witness stand.

You will be asked to state and spell your full name. Even if the clerk does not ask you to spell your last name, it is appropriate to do so for the judge. Frequently, there will be a court reporter taking down all of the testimony using a small machine that looks like a mini-typewriter. Since the witness stand is elevated, the reporter will be located slightly below you, directly in front of the witness stand or off to one side. The reporter will be looking at you regularly to check for pronunciation and to get the rhythm of your speech. Be certain to consider this individual. When talking about anything of a technical nature or mentioning unusual names, stop and spell them for the reporter. The reporter has a great deal of latitude and power in the courtroom. Do not talk too fast or the reporter will interrupt, which will impede the flow of your answers. Speak in a loud, calm, and firm voice and look directly at the individual asking the question.

Testifying in a custody matter usually does not involve a jury trial. However, there are some states, like Texas, where this might take place. Even when testifying before a jury, the witness should still look at the individual asking the questions and *not* at the jury. It makes most jurors uncomfortable to be spoken to directly, and it is better that they feel more like observers and eavesdroppers rather than participants. Many will disagree with this position, so it is wise to consult with the attorney as to how s/he wants you to deal with the jury.

The same theoretical position applies to testifying before a judge. When taking your seat it is certainly appropriate and permissible to smile at the judge, nod, and let him or her know that you recognize his or her presence. Do not talk directly to the judge unless s/he asks you a specific question. Judges will often ask questions in custody matters as they may wish to follow-up on some area that they feel may not have been adequately covered.

The cardinal rule of testifying in court is to *never become angry on the witness stand*. Never argue with an attorney or make snide or sarcastic statements. An attorney addressing you in a hostile or patronizing manner or tone is deliberately trying to make you lose your composure. Rise above this: listen to the words only and ignore the "music." Never make jokes with the attorney unless something is said that is funny to everyone. The courtroom is not the place for snappy banter. However, there is so much tension in court that humor often does sneak in. This serves to break the tension and allows things to proceed. This can be enjoyed but should never be exploited.

There is nothing wrong with politely contradicting an attorney, or disagreeing. This must be done calmly and not in a hostile, annoyed, or perturbed manner. If an attorney has no respect for you, this is the time to have respect for him or her. The judge has seen all of the "games" attorneys play many hundreds of times. You will impress the judge far more and make your points more effectively if you refuse to be drawn into them.

Dress is most important in the courtroom. In my office I rarely wear a tie or jacket. In court, though, I am always dressed in a suit and tie. When you present yourself in court you are representing both yourself and your position. The impression you intend to make must be geared to enhance your most positive side. Men should always wear a jacket and tie, and women a dress or suit. Although I have seen women wearing pants in court, they are not as appropriate as a dress. The court may not be overly strict regarding dress but your appearance can establish a positive, business-like attitude and this should be remembered at all times.

The courtroom should not be thought of as a terribly threatening place. It demands a professional attitude, a slightly formal air, and a level emotional tone. If these areas are mastered, the presentation will go well and the data will have its desired effect. Above all, you want to be believed. Deviating from accepted norms and rules has the effect of neutralizing what you have to say and will be counterproductive.

Preparing to be a Witness

For the professional psychologist or any other expert witness, there is an art to being an effective witness. One can prepare for testifying and do exceptionally well if specific guidelines are followed. As parents read these guidelines for professionals, they can pick up a great many tips on how to be an effective lay witness as well. Most consider the court experience an ordeal but it need not be traumatic if the individual knows the inner workings of the art of witnessing.

The most basic statement that can be made with regard to preparation is that the expert witness should know the case inside and out. In court there should be no material that comes as a surprise. Everything should be thought out before the court appearance, understood thoroughly, and answered completely. This may sound like a difficult order but the professional witness must remember that s/he is an "expert." Therefore, s/he has the responsibility of being the most knowledgeable person on the subject of that particular custody problem.

Nine basic steps need to be taken for effective and thorough preparation. They are straightforward, easy to do, and should be followed without exception. If all nine steps are followed correctly, the courtroom experience will always be gratifying and exciting rather than fearful and traumatic.

1. Read your report thoroughly before coming into court. When asked questions in court, you must be prepared to deliver your answers in an extemporaneous and confident manner. This means that you cannot take the time to fish through your report to see what you said. Know the report. The report should be in front of you on the witness stand but it is important that you have read it before witnessing. Make a one-page outline of the most important points, dates, times, problems of the parents, and needs of the children. Type this in upper case and have it on top of the report in front of you. Try to anticipate what might come up, and have those points elaborated already so that they are clear in your memory and can be recalled instantly. Recognize vague statements and contradictions in your report, and be prepared to clarify and discuss these in detail. They will undoubtedly come up in cross-examination and your job will be to demonstrate how well you know the situation and everything that you have said on the subject.

2. Review the data thoroughly so that you are comfortable in discussing various responses, their meanings, and alternative interpretations. On your single sheet synopsis be certain that you list the tests you used. You should have a brief (two or three sentence) description of each test memorized and ready to discuss. On cross-examination a bright attorney might ask what a certain test purports to measure, why you used it in this matter, when it was standardized, and what the data reveals. Do not underestimate attorneys. They do their homework and you must be able to show your expertise is superior to theirs. You must know your tests and what they measure because you *will* be questioned on this point. If you attempt to avoid this area by not administering any tests, you will be attacked for that. When tests are utilized, the psychologist should have a detailed body of information about the kinds of responses elicited and their interpretations.

3. Be prepared to defend your data with references and points of authority. When I come into court I often bring with me lists of references supporting the tests I have used in the custody evaluation. The attorney cross-examining you will have references supplied by his or her psychological consultant to indicate the poor reliability or validity of your tests and data. You must have counter information so that you can demonstrate the worth of these instruments in a professional manner. The judge may not be familiar with the psychological tests and should have an opportunity to see your expertise with regard to why you selected and how you used these instruments. Do not hesitate to bring reference books, texts, the diagnostic nomenclature manuals, or any other book with you on the stand. You may never need to use these sources but they can serve as useful backup material and also as a means of intimidating the attorney who wishes to attack you.

4. Be prepared to discuss all of the possible alternatives for this custody situation—other than the one you have chosen. When an attorney questions you on the possibility of other answers to the custody problem, it must become apparent to the judge that you have thoroughly considered these options, and rejected them prior to arriving at your own recommendation. I have seen many psychologists questioned in this way who have said, "Well, I hadn't thought of that alternative—it might work; I don't really know." This type of testimony severely compromises your credibility. The judge may conclude that if you have not considered all the possibilities, then perhaps your entire testimony is invalid. When an alternative is brought up, you must be prepared to say, "I did entertain that possibility, but based on X, Y, and Z data, I rejected it." This type of decisiveness gives more credence to your testimony, holds the judge's interest, and presents you as a definitive individual with a clear message. Of course, in order to do this, you must do your homework thoroughly, and reason out beforehand why other forms of custody would not be appropriate for this case. All alternatives must be studied and eliminated so that you have a solid position to present.

5. Use language indicating certainty with regard to your conclusions. Do not hedge or waffle. Attorneys who are good at cross-examination will ask their question, answer it themselves, and then try to get you to endorse the answer. Recently in court, an attorney asked a question, suggested that nobody could possibly answer it, and then said to me in a very friendly tone, "Well, it really looks like a Catch-22, doesn't it Doctor?" It would have been easy to just flow with the drift and agree; however, it is important to state firmly, "No, not at all because. . . ." Be clear in your statements. Even if you agree with the attorney, restate the position in your own language. If you disagree, say so directly. Attorneys may attempt to intimidate you with their tone, body posture, facial expression, or other distracting behavior. Attorneys will also try to fool you by professing ignorance or by professing expertise. It is most important to listen to their questions carefully, and avoid being trapped by any of their extra-curricular games. A court proceeding is replete with games and techniques. Be familiar with them and prepare yourself. Do not allow an attorney to put words into your mouth by couching it in the form of a question on another related issue. Rather than answer this question, it is wise to first correct the attorney. Firm and direct language will assist you in making your testimony carry weight.

6. Know the statements that should be heard by the judge, and be certain that you include them in your testimony. No matter what questions are asked, you must be prepared to get your specific points across. If the "right" questions are not asked, it is up to you to bring forth the information you think is vital. It is certainly very possible to answer a question in an obtuse manner in order to bring in another point and get it heard, but the attorney representing the parent you support should know the correct questions to ask so that your testimony can come across in a strong and positive manner. Do not hesitate to give the attorney a list of questions so that you can be certain that you have an opportunity to completely state your case on behalf of the child. The attorney will usually welcome this, and it will help you to present your data logically and concisely. You want the judge to hear everything that supports your position.

7. Organize your material carefully. It is very rare for an attorney to come into court with a simple manila folder with the client's name and number. Instead, the attorney has been trained to have all data, depositions, supportive information, and questions carefully outlined, filed, and ready for easy access. Why then shouldn't a psychologist be just as prepared? A psychologist should organize a case file in a binder, with all of the material clearly labeled. This is not to suggest that all cases in the office should be done in this manner, but in court it is extremely helpful to have everything easily accessible. This not only helps you to get to your material quickly when it is needed, but it is also an excellent way to review the case and prepare yourself. The binder may be divided into material that comes from outside of your office (declarations, written histories provided by the clients, lawyers' letters, previous court documents, etc.), and material that comes from inside the office (raw data, notes, reports, letters, etc.). If they are all very clearly indexed and marked you can refer to any of the material quickly without fumbling on the stand. If the case comes up again and requires additional evaluations or testimony, you already have everything organized in a meaningful order. It is also a very good idea to write a one-page summary for each category of material and place it on top of the specific material. By using this method you will have everything clearly developed and will know all of the points you wish to make.

8. Be fluent with the law involved. Attorneys will expect you to know their idiom. They will expect you to be able to talk with them in terms of the law involved in the specific issues of the case. Do the reading and research so that you will be able to make sense and think straight. Ask the attorney in the pretrial conference to explain the issues to you in detail if you do not understand them. Be certain that when you get on the witness stand you are comfortable with your material, the laws, and the areas the attorneys will want to addresss. As the representative of the child, it is critical that your views are heard and respected. In order to act as an effective advocate, you must deliver your message within the context of the legal issues. You must also present your material with decisiveness, forthrightness, and clarity. Effective preparation in the laws involved will enable you to accomplish this.

9. Know your own credentials well. If you are not well-known in the courtroom, you will be asked to discuss your background and your professional credentials. It is a good idea to present your resume to both attorneys if they do not know you. You may also attach a resume to the report you forward to the court so that the judge can learn who you are as well. Be prepared to be attacked whatever your credentials. If you do not have a forensic diploma you will be attacked. If you have it, the attorney will make the point that it doesn't really matter.

7

Mediating Custody Agreements

Bringing People Together

Most attorneys will agree that if a court-ordered psychological evaluation does not uphold their client's position, their chances of winning the case are diminished. If they have been suing for sole custody, they will usually consult thoroughly with their clients and begin to discuss possible alternatives. When the psychological evaluation concludes that a joint custodial arrangement is a better solution, the attorneys for both sides and the parents can all be winners if they can back away from the struggle, work out their differences, and come to an agreement with which they can live. I have seen few situations that would work without some form of mediation. The adversarial mind-set is very hard to break, which is why a third party is often needed to induce the sides to compromise.

When an evaluation recommends a time-sharing, coparenting custody agreement, this option should be carefully explored before proceeding with the case. The parents will need to utilize the services of a mediator with the understanding that they may consult with their attorneys. However, they can also circumvent the legal process by working out the problem themselves. Most people find this to be a very attractive option for a number of reasons: First, they can have a direct voice in their custody decision; second, they do not have to trust a judge, who is an unknown person, with a decision that could affect each member of the family for life; third, they usually feel good about the evaluation because they have had the opportunity to express all of their wishes. Rather than go to the courthouse and attempt to beat each other into oblivion, it is far better to return to the evaluator or go to a mediator for further consultation with regard to contracting.

When parents agree to come in to work out a contract, their first goal should be to understand that their personal feelings about each other have no real consequence to the issue. Instead, it must be very clear in their minds that their job is to switch the entire focus to the needs and future of their child. They must think of what will be best for their child, not who has to supply support or who has to make sacrifices. Focusing on the child puts both parents on an equal basis, allowing them to drop their guard and think in a very different manner. In the past they might have been forced to think aggressively and defensively. Now they can think creatively and caringly.

Once the parents realize that they are not on a battleground but instead on neutral territory, there are often frequent sighs of relief, smiles, and the beginnings of excellent cooperation. They might deteriorate at times during the mediation sessions to engage in petty arguments. Gestures, looks, and complaints set people off and they may begin to argue again. This should not be tolerated. The mediator should stop such bickering immediately by restating the purpose of the meeting, reminding the parties that they are there to deal with the future of their child and *not* with their own past.

During the first half hour of the first mediation session, I do not permit the parents to talk to each other directly. All communications must be directed through me. The parents are not permitted to answer or respond to each other. In this session we discuss only what they expect from their child and what they wish for the child's future. There is very little room for dis-agreement in this area since the underlying assumption is that both parents love the child and want the best for him or her. This initial session is usually quite successful, since it permits the parents to walk out of the office with many basic agree-ments. Careful notes are taken during the session, summarized, and reviewed at the end of the hour. The parents feel good, certain that they have accomplished something worthwhile. They even begin to feel that perhaps the ex-spouse may be a person with whom they can work, and they look forward to the next session.

The second session is scheduled within one or two days after the first, so that the momentum and the positive feelings can be preserved. At the second session the first order of business is to present each parent with the first two pages of the con-tract. In it, I review their basic agreement about what they want for their child, and we go through it again point by point to reinforce it. Speaking as a parent, I outline many of the goals I have always wanted for my own children and expect that most parents want for theirs. Putting it in such a context, it is relatively easy to move the parents into achieving a fundamental agreement. They usually are now thoroughly into the negotiation mode and begin to feel like winners all the way. We then begin to address the actual time-sharing procedures, and we set up dates and times when each parent will have the child. Although some areas are fairly flexible, very little of the contract is kept vague. We deal with areas of support, school, medical care, clothing, bank ac-counts, travel, respect for each other's lifestyle, remedies for breach of contract, and other areas that may be particular to the specific child and family. The parents slowly began to make peace and start offering each other more time in order to make things easier. When the child is to be with one parent for a special Sunday event, the other parent may volunteer to bring the child over on Saturday evening. These types of conciliatory offers and compromises are not unusual at this stage of the mediation procedure.

During the negotiation sessions, the psychologist must be highly vigilant and observant of the slightest nuances between the couple. If the negative statements begin to flow once again, they must be stopped immediately. The parents should realize that this is not the time or place to work out their marriage. Instead, they must see that it is long past, over, finished, and not relevant to this process before them. These negotiation sessions typically must include constant reminders as to the purpose of the meeting: to deal with the future life of the child, and not the parent's individual gripes.

An entire custody contract can usually be written within three to four hours. Initially, when I began conducting these sessions, it would take ten to twelve hours to hammer out the concepts. Now I am able to move the parents through it faster by offering a fairly tight structure to the areas they need to address. After we have come to a final conclusion, the contract is written into final, legal form, and both parents get a copy, as do their attorneys. I urge the parents to remember that they must get their attorneys' advice but I also urge them to remember that this mediation process is by its nature an alternative to court proceedings. I instruct the parents that they have to make very clear to their lawyers exactly what they want for their child. They must keep uppermost in their minds the idea that they cannot be forced back into the legal process if they do not wish to be. Therefore, they each must make considerable and real concessions, and their attorneys must understand this as well. If this can happen, it can neutralize the adversary posture of the participants. After the contract is completely finished, one of the attorneys will file it, the judge will sign it, and it is the order of the court.

The final contract is a fairly tight document written for a specific period of time. It requires a certain amount of follow-up and re-evaluation. The parents usually feel good about having an ongoing relationship with the evaluator, and this fact is written into the contract. When a contract is put into practice and works well, the parents progress in their ability to cooperate since they see their child thriving. As this happens and things continue to work, the parents often do not have to return for periodic evaluations.

In my experience, approximately 90 percent of the contracts continue for unlimited periods of time. The remaining 10 percent deteriorate due to anger, jealousy, money difficulties, and outside interference that usually comes from vindictive grandparents. My experience clearly demonstrates that it is far more productive for parents to engage in the contracting process than to return to court over and over again. The constructive climate inherent to the mediation process reflects positively in the emotional environment of the child, who is spared the antagonism and anxiety that are a natural part of the legal confrontations.

The initial part of the custody contract is quite basic. As indicated, it lists all of the goals and values a caring parent would like to see in a child. Since there is such overwhelming and unanimous agreement on these fundamentals, I use a similar version of this section in almost every contract. I have not yet found any parents whose goals for their child were so totally divergent that this section could not be used.

From this point the negotiation process usually moves swiftly. Parents must be careful not to permit the negotiator to spoon-feed them all of their ideas. They should develop the statements themselves with the guidance and structure offered by the psychologist or mediator. Each concept should be discussed in broad terms before specific wording is suggested. With such a therapeutic approach, parents can learn to deal with even the most difficult areas and find agreement. Parents enjoy producing the custody contract since it empowers them to solve the custody issue by themselves. This permits them truly to decide their own fate and the fate of their child. They do not have to take the chance of leaving this to a judge who might make a very strange, arbitrary, or totally unwarranted decision, as has sometimes occurred in the past.

Sample Contract: Joint Legal and Joint Physical Custody

The first sample contract presented in this section is the product of the Jones Family, who were introduced earlier in the psychological report in this book. The family initially began their time-sharing on a two-week basis with the goal of extending it to two months by the end of the contract. As I write, they have extended the time period to three months, and the child is continuing to thrive and blossom. The parents are very happy with their child and have become fairly good friends. The petty arguments have completely subsided and they have developed a trustful and very business-like attitude toward each other. This has been most productive and continues to support the joint custody situation. They consult with each other, listen to ideas, and make frequent compromises. There is no doubt that the contracting process has worked very well for the Jones family, and over the years they have continued to renew their agreement.

SUPERIOR COURT OF THE STATE OF CALIFORNIA
FOR THE COUNTY OF VENTURA

In re the Marriage of:	)	CASE NO. A 111111
PETITIONER:	)	
BLANCHE D. JONES	)	STIPULATION AND AGREEMENT
and	)	JOINT LEGAL AND PHYSICAL
RESPONDENT:	)	CUSTODY OF MINOR CHILD
NEVILLE D. JONES	)	JAMES O. JONES
————————	)	

STIPULATION:

IT IS HEREBY STIPULATED between the Petitioner BLANCHE D. JONES and the Respondent NEVILLE D. JONES that the parties agree to the joint legal and physical custody of the minor child as follows.

TERM OF CONTRACT:

1. That the parties desire a joint legal and physical custody agreement for the benefit of their minor child JAMES O. JONES and that this agreement shall be effective the 1st day of November 1980 and extend for a period of four years until 1 November 1984.

AGREEMENT TO WITHDRAW ACTION:

2. This agreement is not a compromise arising out of any legal threat or action, but instead it is a measure of good faith, respect, and fair play between these people. They recognize that the central focus of this situation is their child, and they agree to do those things that have been determined to be in his best interests. Agreement to these conditions necessitates the withdrawal of any legal action involving custody. Both parties stipulate to the following conditions:

REQUIREMENTS: RE: JAMES:

3. Petitioner and Respondent both agree as follows:

A. They desire that James shall grow to be a physically healthy, emotionally happy, and spiritually mature person who will be able to cope well with life;

B. They desire that James shall be proud and accepting of himself, his intellect, his gender, his body, his emotions, and that he will develop an independence based on respect for his worth as a person;

C. They desire that James shall grow to be an individual who is highly capable of contributing to society;

D. They desire that James shall be capable of accepting responsibility for his actions and that he will have insight and awareness into alternative modes of responding to life's situations;

E. They desire that James will be provided with all possible opportunities to reach his maximum individual academic potential;

F. They desire that James shall maintain a high quality of classroom study, interest, curiosity, and creativity;

G. They desire that James shall have no barriers to the appropriate expression of both positive and negative feelings;

H. They desire that James will take part in appropriate physical activities;

I. They desire that James will have an awareness and a basic respect for the rights and property of others, be able to follow directions correctly, learn to listen effectively, exercise self-control, and use cooperation skills with others;

J. They desire that James will utilize his time carefully so that he may participate in a balance of activities including eating, sleeping, and other daily routines such as chores, schoolwork, family and home activities, as well as music, sports, religious activities, and quiet time of his own which may be unstructured;

K. They desire that James shall be honest and open with his feelings;

L. They desire that James shall be respectful to each parent, grandparent, and stepparent, and that he shall relate very effectively with all family members;

M. They desire that James shall be granted time to pursue his own special interests. They recognize that he requires enrichment, stimulation, and time with each parent in both fun as well as educational activities. They also recognize that he will require time alone for more solitary and personal interests and activities.

JOINT LEGAL, JOINT PHYSICAL CUSTODY STATEMENT:

4. Having agreed upon the above goals, the Petitioner and Respondent, in an effort to provide and maintain for James a healthy and stable lifestyle, do hereby stipulate that a joint legal and physical custody agreement will exist with each parent having a voice in major decisions regarding the growth, development, and education of the child. The Petitioner and Respondent will consult with each other, respect each other's opinions, and make joint decisions whenever it is possible in these areas. If either parent should perceive any major upset in the child, that parent will discuss the situation [with the other] prior to taking any specific action. Neither parent has the right to dictate to the other, but instead, consultation is encouraged so that perceptions and feelings can be shared and discussed.

RESIDENCE OF PARTIES:

5. Petitioner and Respondent agree that they will maintain a joint physical custody relationship with their child. They understand that this may not always constitute an equal fifty percent distribution of time. Petitioner and Respondent both express their desire to maintain a California residence as their principle place of domicile. Should either of them contemplate a change of residence to another county within the same state or to another state, that person shall notify the other parent in writing at least thirty days prior to the move.

CUSTODY CYCLES:

6. Both parties agree that the joint physical custody relationship will be established as follows: Initially, a two-week cycle will exist. The first week of November, 1980 (beginning on Sunday, the second day of November) is designated as PHASE ONE. Phase One will extend for two weeks and will terminate on Sunday, 16 November at 9:00 A.M. PHASE TWO will then begin and extend to Sunday, 30 November at 9:00 A.M.

On Sunday, 2 November at 9:00 A.M., Petitioner will bring James to Respondent and James will remain there for the Phase

One period. During this time Petitioner will have visitation each Wednesday evening from 4:00 P.M. to 8:00 P.M. Petitioner shall also have James each Sunday from 9:00 A.M. to 6:00 P.M. Respondent will return James to Petitioner on Sunday, 16 November at 9:00 A.M. for Phase Two at which time the Petitioner has custody and Respondent has visitation. In each instance, the parent who has the custody of James will deliver him to the other parent. For the month of November there will be no flexibility in this schedule. At the end of Phase Two, the schedule will extend itself to one month with each parent and after six of these rotations, a two-month schedule will be adopted. At that time a re-evaluation will take place in order to ensure that a continuous and regular two-month system can be established successfully.

NON-INVOLVEMENT AGREEMENT:

7. Each party mutually covenants and agrees that they recognize that they are divorced, and that they will not be directly involved in each other's lives at any time. They shall accord one to the other the necessary respect, cooperation, and calmness in order to carry out the terms and conditions of this agreement throughout all of their communications, be they oral or written.

CONDITIONS:

8. Petitioner and Respondent agree to provide all conditions that are necessary in order to support the goals as outlined above. This includes appropriate conditions for sleep, play, and schoolwork. James is to have regular routines so that his needs can be met in a reasonable manner.

CHANGEOVER RULES:

9. Both parties covenant and agree to prepare James for the changeover times in both the physical and emotional modes. He is to be kept aware of the changeover or visitation schedule. He will be permitted to take any of his personal articles including

toys, school supplies, and clothes from one home to the other without restrictions. The Petitioner and Respondent will be equally responsible for clothes. They each agree to have fourteen days supply of clothes on hand which they will buy independently. Large items such as coats or shoes will be purchased jointly and expenses will be shared. Any other special fees such as specific lessons will be discussed prior to incurring these fees and then shared jointly on agreement between the parties.

FUTURE SUPPORT:

10. Both Petitioner and Respondent agree that child support payments will be waived at this time. Both parties agree to establish a trust account at a recognized California savings institution as follows: Neville D. Jones and Blanche D. Jones, Cust. for James O. Jones (Cust. F/Minor UGTMA Calif.). They further agree to make regular deposits into that account of not less than $50.00 each month by each parent. In this manner they are declaring a continuing interest in their child and they are agreed that these funds will be utilized solely for James's future educational advancement.

HEALTH INSURANCE:

11. Both parties agree to cover James with their own individual private health insurance plans. They will provide each other with claim forms and alert the insurance companies to their dual coverage.

SPECIAL DAYS:

12. James will spend Father's Day with his father and Mother's Day with his mother. The parents will not deviate from the schedule but instead, the custodial parent will deliver James for the day (9:00 A.M. to 6:00 P.M.). On James's birthday the non-custodial parent will be permitted to see him for at least a two-hour period during the day whenever possible.

HOLIDAY SCHEDULE:

13. During the term of this contract all major holidays shall be shared equally. Christmas will be split with both parents: James will celebrate Christmas Day with Petitioner on all even years and with Respondent on all odd years. Thanksgiving Day will be alternated as well and James will celebrate with Petitioner on all odd years and with Respondent on all even years. Easter will be split in half each year. Summer schedules will not deviate from the normal changeovers.

TELEPHONE COMMUNICATION:

14. During James's period of cohabitation with the custodial parent, the noncustodial parent shall have the right to communicate with him by telephone every other evening for a maximum period of ten minutes. Both parties will reveal their telephone numbers to each other, and they agree and covenant that at no time will they abuse this information or permit others to abuse this information.

MEDICAL CARE:

15. Each parent will alert the other with regard to medical appointments, illnesses, or medical attention necessary for James. In the event of any life-threatening emergencies, medical care will be given immediately and then the custodial parent will notify the other as soon as possible. James will continue to see his present physician.

EDUCATIONAL INFORMATION ACCESS:

16. At all times both parents will have access to information regarding James's education as well as information from parent/teacher conferences. The pupil emergency notification cards submitted to the school will have both parents listed. Both parties agree to cooperate in all of James's educational needs, and they further agree to see that all homework and special projects are considered with regular time periods set aside so that they can be successfully accomplished. When special activities come up such

as school plays, open house, or graduations, the custodial parent will extend the courtesy of notifying the other parent. Both parents, parents' partners, stepparents, or grandparents are welcome to attend these activities. James will be informed of this so that he does not get apprehensive with regard to possible friction between the parents.

CHOICES OF CHILD:

17. Both parties covenant and agree to respect choices made by James so that his attendance in school and other enrichment activities shall be duly considered in any decision-making process.

DEROGATORY REMARKS:

18. Both parties covenant and agree that they shall not make any derogatory remarks or comments to James about each other's lifestyle or parenting skills. They shall not permit any other type of derogatory remark (demonstrated by gesture, expression, or verbal statements) to be made about each other in James's presence by any other person.

LOG BOOK COMMUNICATION:

19. Petitioner and Respondent agree to maintain a log book. This log book will consist of a journal in which parents will communicate with each other with regard to their child and his needs. Parents will write questions, information, things to watch for, activity schedules, medication schedules, and positive statements. They will not write complaints about each other to each other. They are to keep uppermost in their minds that the log book is a specific vehicle for the process of communicating about the child only. The journal is to be exchanged at the visitation times to enhance effective communication. Parents only shall write in this log book.

FLEXIBILITY, MEDIATION:

20. Both parties agree that they will do all in their power to be flexible and respectful of each other so that any minor

disagreements do not escalate. If a disagreement does take place, the parties agree that they will discuss the issues carefully and seek mediation or arbitration services if necessary for resolution of the problem.

COMMITMENT TO ONGOING CONTRACT:

21. Both parties covenant and agree that they intend to continue and maintain joint legal and physical custody of their child. To this end they both agree that at the termination of this contract they will either renegotiate or extend the contract.

FOCUS ON CHILD:

22. Both parties do covenant and agree to place the welfare of their child uppermost in their minds. They agree to enter into this stipulation in an unselfish, cooperative, and positive state of mind. They will, to the best of their abilities, be honest and reasonable. During the period of this agreement, they will support James's relationship with parents, grandparents, and stepparents.

CONSULTATIONS:

23. Each party will support this stipulation in a dedicated and concerned manner. Both parties agree to regular consultations with Dr. Diamond (or other agreed-upon counselor) to review any ideas, difficulties, or potential problems. These consultations will take place at approximately six-month intervals.

BREACHES, REMEDIES:

24. If either party feels that a serious breach of this contract has taken place, that individual is to consult with Dr. Diamond prior to taking any legal action. Both parties agree that they will do all in their power to be flexible in their thoughts and actions. They also agree to be respectful of each other so that minor disagreements do not escalate into full-blown, wasteful court action. If a disagreement does occur, the parties agree to utilize the mediation procedures. It is also agreed that if it is

determined that James requires any psychological treatment, this will be attended to in a cooperative manner.

FEES:

25. Each party agrees to pay one-half of all fees due to Leonard Diamond, Ph.D., for all consultations and for the final preparation of this contract. Any other subsequent fees herein incurred shall also be shared between the parties on an equal basis for any joint consultations.

26. This document addresses itself only to the custody of the minor child and not to any other stipulations which are in full force and effect and based in legal action. This document, as prepared by Dr. Diamond, is a psychological contract which has been arrived at through specific scientific psychological and mediation techniques, and should in no way be viewed as the work product of an attorney.

APPROVED AS TO FORM AND CONTENT:

_____   _____
BLANCHE D. JONES, PETITIONER   DATED:

_____   _____
NEVILLE D. JONES, RESPONDENT   DATED:

_____   _____
ATTORNEY FOR THE PETITIONER   DATED:

_____   _____
ATTORNEY FOR THE RESPONDENT   DATED:

ORDER

The Court having reviewed the above stipulation and agreement hereby ORDERS, ADJUDGES, and DECREES that all terms and conditions contained therein shall be the order of the court forthwith, and each party shall be ordered to comply with all terms and conditions.

_____

JUDGE OF THE SUPERIOR COURT

Sample Contract: Joint Legal but Sole Physical Custody

Although great geographical distances between parents can be very difficult to overcome, they can be bridged with custody contracts, which can be especially successful when dealing with older children. These circumstances involve changing schools and should not be dealt with lightly. Whether such custody agreements should be effected is very much dependent on the skills, abilities, and flexibility of the individual child. Younger children usually require longer periods of time to get adjusted to a new school and a drastic change could adversely affect their learning skills. In the case of the following contract, a mother was planning to move to another part of the state to take advantage of an occupational opportunity for herself. She intended to take her daughter, and a bitter court battle ensued with many restraining orders, claims, charges, and countercharges. The parents were referred to a mediator by the court as a last resort. A joint agreement was worked out with an equal distribution of time to both parents until the child began elementary school. At that point she was to be in the sole custody of her mother. This contract works equally well with parents of either gender receiving sole custody. It is offered to demonstrate the intricacies of working out a very concrete agreement regarding time distribution.

This contract is working very well since the couple is highly cooperative. Prior to coming in, they thought only in terms of winning or losing. Their attorneys and the judge cooperated in helping to educate them about the need to concentrate on the best interests of the child. Once the mediation process began, they actually realized that they should be thinking about and working for their daughter. Their anger subsided and they worked in a productive and cooperative manner. It is my opinion that this arrangement will continue to work. Parents work well with such a structure. The contracting process offers a degree more comfort, and the understanding that any breach of the contract might result is a full-blown, expensive, and complex court battle acts as a restraint. Court is the costliest and the least desirable option.

SUPERIOR COURT OF THE STATE OF CALIFORNIA FOR THE COUNTY OF VENTURA

In re the Marriage of:)   **CASE NO. B 222222**
PETITIONER:)
JILL SMITH   ) STIPULATION AND AGREEMENT
   and   ) JOINT LEGAL, SOLE PHYSICAL
RESPONDENT:) CUSTODY OF MINOR CHILD
JACK SMITH   ) JENNY SMITH
—————————————)

STIPULATION:

IT IS HEREBY STIPULATED between the Petitioner JILL SMITH and the Respondent JACK SMITH that the parties agree to the joint legal and sole physical custody of the minor child as follows.

DESIRES OF THE PARTIES:

1. That the parties desire an agreement for the benefit of their minor child JENNY SMITH. This agreement shall be effective the 1st day of April 1989 and continue to December 1993 at which time it will be re-evaluated.

PARAMETERS OF AGREEMENT:

2. This agreement is not a compromise arising out of any legal threat or action, but instead is a measure of good faith, respect, and fair play between these people. They recognize that the central focus of this situation is their child, and they agree to do those things that have been determined to be in her best interests. Agreement to these conditions necessitates the withdrawal of any legal action involving custody. Both parties stipulate to the following conditions:

AGREEMENTS RE: JENNY:

3. Petitioner and Respondent both agree as follows:

A. They desire that Jenny shall grow to be a physically healthy, emotionally happy, and spiritually mature person who will be able to cope well with life;

B. They desire that Jenny shall be proud and accepting of herself, her intellect, her gender, her body, her emotions, and that she will develop an independence based on respect for her worth as a person;

C. They desire that Jenny shall grow to be an individual who is highly capable of contributing to society;

D. They desire that Jenny shall be capable of accepting responsibility for her actions and that she will have insight and awareness into alternative modes of responding to life's situations;

E. They desire that Jenny will be provided with all possible opportunities to reach her maximum individual academic potential;

F. They desire that Jenny shall maintain a high quality of classroom study, interest, curiosity, and creativity;

G. They desire that Jenny will be capable of appropriately expressing both positive and negative feelings;

H. They desire that Jenny will take part in appropriate physical activities;

I. They desire that Jenny will have an awareness and a basic respect for the rights and property of others, be able to follow directions correctly, learn to listen effectively, exercise self-control, and use cooperation skills with others;

J. They desire that Jenny will utilize her time carefully so that she may participate in a balance of activities including eating, sleeping, and other daily routines such as chores, schoolwork, family and home activities, as well as music, sports, religious activities, and quiet time of her own which may be unstructured;

K. They desire that Jenny shall be honest and open with her feelings;

L. They desire that Jenny shall be respectful to each parent, grandparent, and stepparent, and that she shall relate very effectively with all family members;

M. They desire that Jenny shall be granted time to pursue her own special interests. They recognize that she requires enrichment, stimulation, and time with each parent in both fun as well as educational activities. They also recognize that she will require time alone for more solitary and personal interests and activities.

JOINT LEGAL, SOLE PHYSICAL CUSTODY STATEMENT:

4. Having agreed upon the above goals, the Petitioner and Respondent, in an effort to provide and maintain for Jenny a healthy and stable lifestyle, do hereby stipulate to the following conditions:

Both parties covenant and agree that a joint legal custody agreement will exist between them. Each parent will have a voice in major decisions regarding education, growth, and development of the child. They will consult each other and they will exchange information regarding Jenny's development on a regular basis;

Both parties agree that Petitioner shall be granted sole physical custody of Jenny. Petitioner agrees that under no circumstances will she move out of the State of California unless agreed to in writing by Respondent. She is permitted to move to northern California while Respondent continues to reside in southern California.

CUSTODY CYCLES:
5. Time-sharing will be as follows:

April 01, 1989 - April 16, 1989	Respondent
April 16, 1989 - June 04, 1989	Petitioner
June 04, 1989 - July 16, 1989	Respondent
July 16, 1989 - Aug. 27, 1989	Petitioner
Aug. 27, 1989 - Oct. 08, 1989	Respondent
Oct. 08, 1989 - Nov. 19, 1989	Petitioner
Nov. 19, 1989 - Dec. 03, 1989	Respondent
Dec. 03, 1989 - Jan. 01, 1990	Petitioner
January and February 1990	Respondent
March, April, and May 1990	Petitioner
June and July 1990	Respondent
August, September and October 1990	Petitioner
November and December 1990	Respondent
January, February, and March 1991	Petitioner
April and May 1991	Respondent
June 1991	Petitioner
July and August 1991	Respondent

On September 1, 1991, Jenny will be returned to Petitioner. At that time Jenny will begin elementary school. She will remain in the custody of Petitioner, and Respondent will have visitations for Easter vacations and alternate Christmas vacations. Respondent will also have visitation on alternate weekends when he is in the geographical area from Fridays at 5:00 P.M. to Sundays at 3:00 P.M. Agreed upon weekday evenings will also be granted on a reasonable basis with advance notice of forty-eight hours. During the time-sharing sequences from April, 1989 through September, 1991, the noncustodial parent shall have the same visitation rights when he or she is in the geographical area.

Both Petitioner and Respondent have agreed to exhibit concern and flexibility so that Jenny will not be denied the opportunity to visit the noncustodial parent. After Jenny begins school, Respondent will have custody from one week after school ends in June to one week before school begins in September. Petitioner will have two uninterrupted weeks of visitation during the summer months at a mutually agreed-upon and convenient time. If Jenny should attend a year-round school program, Respondent will have visitation for four midtrack vacations, Easter vacation, and alternate Christmas vacations. He will also be able to visit on alternate weekends with notice to Petitioner.

DIVORCE AGREEMENT:

6. Each party mutually convenants and agrees that they recognize that they are divorced, and that they will not be directly involved in each other's lives at any time, and shall accord one to the other the necessary cooperation, respect, and calmness in order to carry out the terms and conditions of this agreement throughout all of their communications be they oral or written.

TELEPHONE COMMUNICATION:

7. During Jenny's period of cohabitation with the custodial parent, the noncustodial parent shall have the right to communicate with her by mail with no restrictions. Telephone calls by the noncustodial parent may be made every other evening for a maximum period of ten minutes.

CHOICES OF CHILD:

8. Respondent and Petitioner agreed to provide all conditions

that are necessary in order to support the goals as outlined above. This includes all appropriate conditions for sleep, play, and school-work. Jenny is to have regular routines so that her needs will be met in a reasonable manner.

HEALTH INSURANCE:

9. Both parties covenant and agree that Jenny will be covered by Petitioner's medical insurance. Both Petitioner and Respondent shall be equally responsible for deductible fees, as well as medical, dental, and visual expenses not covered by the existing medical insurance.

CLOTHING:

10. Both parties covenant and agree that they shall each buy clothing for Jenny independently, and they shall assure that they have an adequate supply of clothing on hand. She will also be able to take favored clothes and toys when the exchanges are made. Both parties agree to return all articles to the other parent at the end of the stay. Large and expensive items such as coats and shoes will be purchased jointly.

CHANGEOVER RULES:

11. Both parties covenant and agree to prepare Jenny for the changeover times in both the physical and emotional modes. The parent with custody shall take responsibility for delivering Jenny. This may be accomplished by delivering her to the closest airport (if airplane travel is planned) or one-half way to the other home at a pre-arranged site (if car travel is planned). The parent receiving the custody will buy a meal for both parents and Jenny and they will discuss plans, activities, and schedules in a calm and cooperative manner.

LOG BOOK COMMUNICATION:

12. Petitioner and Respondent shall keep a log book. This log book will consist of a journal in which parents will communicate with each other with regard to their child and her needs.

Parents will write questions, information, things to watch for, activity schedules, and positive statements. They will not write complaints about each other to each other. They are to keep uppermost in their minds that the log book is a specific vehicle for the process of communicating about the child only. The journal is to be exchanged at the visitation times to enhance effective communication. Parents only shall write in the log book. Both parents are encouraged to take pictures and include them in the journal.

MEDICAL CARE:

13. Each parent will alert the other with regard to medical appointments, illnesses, or medical attention necessary for Jenny. In the event of any life-threatening emergencies, medical care will be given immediately and then the custodial parent will notify the other as soon as reasonably possible. The parents will be certain that the physicians who deal with Jenny in each geographical area will share information and exchange medical records on a regular basis.

EDUCATIONAL INFORMATION ACCESS:

14. At all times both parents will have access to information regarding Jenny's education, and information stemming from parent/teacher conferences. Both parents, parents' partners, step-parents, or grandparents are welcome to attend school activities. Jenny shall be informed of this so that she does not get apprehensive with regard to possible friction between her parents.

DEROGATORY REMARKS:

15. Both parties covenant and agree that they shall not make derogatory remarks or comments to Jenny about each other's lifestyle or parenting skills and they shall not permit any other type of derogatory remark about each other to be made in her presence by any other person.

CHILD SUPPORT AGREEMENT:

16. Respondent shall pay to Petitioner the sum of $150.00 per month for child support on or about the first of each month that Petitioner has custody of Jenny.

FUTURE SUPPORT:

17. Both parties agree to establish a trust account at a recognized California financial institution as follows: Jill Smith and Jack Smith, Cust. for Jenny Smith (Cust. F/Minor UGTMA Calif.). They further agree to make regular deposits into that account each month of not less than $20.00 by each parent. In this manner they are declaring a continuing interest in their child, and they are agreed that these funds will be utilized solely for Jenny's future educational advancement.

FLEXIBILITY:

18. Both parties agree that they will do all in their power to be flexible and respectful of each other so that any minor disagreements do not escalate. If a disagreement does take place, the parties agree that they will discuss the issues carefully and seek mediation or arbitration services if necessary for resolution of the problem.

FOCUS ON CHILD:

19. Both parties do covenant and agree to place the welfare of their child uppermost in their minds. They agree to enter into this stipulation in an unselfish, cooperative, and positive state of mind. They will, to the best of their abilities, be honest and reasonable. During the period of this agreement, they will support Jenny's relationship with parents, grandparents, and step-parents. They will make no comments, expressions, gestures, or any statements which may be construed as negative to the other parent.

CONSULTATIONS:

20. Flexibility in this stipulation is advised and it is agreed

that each parent will support the custody situation in a dedicated and concerned manner. Both parties agree to have a yearly consultation with Dr. Diamond (or other agreed-upon counselor) to review any ideas, difficulties, or potential problems. Jenny is to be evaluated psychologically after her kindergarten year and every two years thereafter. A consultation will then be held with both parents to review the data and help to make further plans for Jenny.

BREACHES, REMEDIES:

21. If either party feels that a serious breach of this contract has taken place, that individual is to make an appointment with Dr. Diamond prior to taking any legal action. Both parties agree that they will do all in their power to be flexible in their thoughts and actions. They also agree to be respectful of each other so that minor disagreements do not escalate into full-blown, wasteful court action. If a disagreement should occur, the parties agree to remediate the difficulties through counseling.

SIGNING, FILING:

22. It is agreed that the parties may execute this stipulation in counterpart. It is further agreed that Petititioner will prepare this stipulation for filing in the official court record. Any other financial, property, or support agreements will remain in full force and effort until they are replaced by a future stipulation.

23. This document addresses itself only to the custody of the minor child and not to any other stipulations which are based in legal action. This document, as prepared by Dr. Diamond, is a psychological contract which has been arrived at through specific scientific psychological and mediation techniques, and should in no way be viewed as the work product of an attorney.

APPROVED AS TO FORM AND CONTENT:

_____   _____
JILL SMITH, PETITIONER   JACK SMITH, RESPONDENT

Dated _____   Dated _____

_____   _____
ATTORNEY FOR   ATTORNEY FOR
THE PETITIONER   THE RESPONDENT

Dated _____   Dated _____

ORDER

The Court having reviewed the above stipulation and agreement hereby ORDERS, ADJUDGES and DECREES that all terms and conditions contained therein shall be the order of the court forthwith, and each party shall be ordered to comply with all said terms and conditions.

_____
JUDGE OF THE SUPERIOR COURT

8
Summary

Conclusions: The Future of Custody Matters

Although there can be points of style and content common to all custody contracts, each should be tailored to the individual situation. Contracts can be written for any form of the custody arrangement (joint legal and joint physical; joint legal and sole physical; sole legal and sole physical). Each family presents a different set of problems that must be dealt with individually. Although the need for some "boiler plate" is evident, it is not appropriate to simply offer a "form" contract that is pulled from a drawer with blank spaces for the names and dates.

Contracts can also be highly successful in situations where the parents are separated by significant geographical distances. The key of course, is effective, positive, and creative communication. This hurdle can be overcome by carefully spelling out specific rules for communication. This is done in a rigid and concrete form so that the parents cannot go astray. Once they achieve more positive feelings they can begin to trade ideas, feelings, be more creative, and take over the process. This is the general routine of a successful custody arrangement. I have seen families in which the parents despised each other intensely but were able to work out successful contracts because they could agree that the child was special and loved by both of them. With a written agreement that left little to chance, much of the anger and fear was removed and restructured into creative energy.

The object of this book has been to educate a parent contemplating a custody battle about the inner workings of the courtroom, and the psychological and mediation processes. The field of custody is most difficult for both attorneys and psychologists since these cases are often so volatile. The information in this book should assist a parent to make effective and appropriate plans as s/he pursues custody. The alternative of joint custody is the current preferred position in most enlightened states and it should never be ruled out.

This book has also been written to educate both the psychologist and attorney. The field of custody is difficult, rewarding, and always supplies new material for learning. Each family comes to the attorney and the psychologist with a different set of needs, feelings, problems, and values. They make foolish accusations, play strategy games, and often forget that the object of the dispute is their child. Re-focusing their energy and caring on the child goes a long way toward resolving these circumstances. Just as a custody judgment can never be a final judgment, a custody evalution can never be an absolute answer. Each family is a unique entity. The complexity of needs in individual relationships continually broadens the psychological study of family systems. The world of the family law courtroom offers an exquisite excitement. It is a new forum in which the psychologist is given the opportunity to practice this science on a platform where s/he is respected and where his or her services are actively recruited.

Parents, judges, attorneys, and psychologists continue actively to seek education about custody. It is an emerging area that had been overlooked for many years. Now we are refining skills, and learning to work in a cooperative manner. The work of a custody evaluator is intense and offers an opportunity to make a significant contribution to the lives of children. It must be taken very seriously.

As mentioned previously, the custody area places both the clinical psychologist and the attorney in very visible and vulnerable positions. They need to conduct this type of practice according to the strictest ethical and business principles. Parents must feel they can trust these profesisonals to move them toward correct solutions that are in the best interests of the children.

The future of the field of custody is clear. It is my opinion that the formal litigation process will not survive in this area. Deciding the fate of children and parents is not appropriate in the courtroom but should be done by the parents themselves. The current process will and should be replaced by psychological investigation, mediation, arbitration, and the custody contracting process. This appears to be the most effective manner to deal with the complexity of custody arrangements. It is far more productive than adversarial struggles, court hearings, and judicial pronouncements. Clinical psychologists are now playing an integral role in the process of mediating custody. Family law attorneys must eventually restructure their values so that they can take a position on the side of the child rather than as an advocate for one parent. In concert, judges, mediators, psychologists, and family law attorneys can continue to develop new systems.

Although the legal issue of custody has been well-known for many years, it has been poorly defined and we are all still relative novices in understanding all of the parameters of the parent-child relationship. The information I have presented in this book is an overview of one psychologist's experiences and insights. It is probably far more crude than we realize, but it works well for the present and it is a beginning. It is my hope that this will spark new and more creative thinking, for we need all of the data we can get to propel us ahead onto the next plateau of clearer understanding.